ChangeWave Investing 2.0

Dear Joey
Welcome to the
WAVE
Code Key James!

Picking the Next Monster Stocks While
Protecting Your Gains in a Volatile Market

CHANGEWAVE
INVESTING 2.0

Tobin Smith

Author of *ChangeWave Investing*

CURRENCY

NEW YORK   LONDON   TORONTO   SYDNEY   AUCKLAND

A CURRENCY BOOK
Published by Doubleday
a division of Random House, Inc.
1540 Broadway, New York, New York 10036

Currency and Doubleday are trademarks of Doubleday,
a division of Random House, Inc.

Library of Congress Cataloging-in-Publication Data

Smith, Tobin, 1957–
   ChangeWave investing 2.0 : picking the next monster stocks while protecting
your gains in a volatile market / Tobin Smith.
      p. cm.
   Includes bibliographical references and index.
   ISBN 0-385-50244-3
   1. Investments. 2. Speculation. 3. Stocks.   I. Title.
   HG6041 .S639 2001
   332.63'22—dc21

                                                              2001047164

Book design by Erin L. Matherne and Tina Thompson

PRINTED IN THE UNITED STATES OF AMERICA

First Edition: October 2001

10 9 8 7 6 5 4 3 2 1

Currency Books are available at special discounts for bulk purchases
for sales promotions or premiums. Special editions, including personalized
covers, excerpts of existing books, and corporate imprints, can be created in
large quantities for special needs. For more information, write to Special Markets,
Currency Books, 280 Park Avenue, 11th floor, New York, NY 10017,
or email *specialmarkets@randomhouse.com.*

To PCS,
whose relentless support and unconditional love
allowed me to dream big dreams.

CONTENTS

ACKNOWLEDGMENTS

ChangeWave is about one thing: helping people profit from change. In that spirit, there have been many individuals who've been instrumental in changing this simple mission into both a book and a worldwide community of more than 250,000 people, since our launch in June 2000.

Thanks go first to Carol Susan Roth, my agent, who had the unmitigated gall to round up the best business publishers in the world and land us with the best. Doubleday Currency's Roger Scholl is owed a debt of gratitude for the belief and support required to bring the ChangeWave message to all the corners of the world (in eight languages and CD, no less!)

A very significant debt is owed to the ChangeWave Investment Research LLC team, especially the editorial efforts of Dan Gainor, Chris Wachtelhausen, and Sam Collins, in getting this book to the finish line. My apologies to all for the many times my door was closed to all as I pounded this latest edition of our philosophy and strategies to meet deadlines. Special gratitude as well goes to the founding members of Change-Wave: Dave Durham, John Baldwin, Nick Moccia, Mark Anderson, Cindy Leach, and Paul Carton for their tireless devotion to our quest.

Thanks to Tom Phillips, chairman of Phillips International, and John Coyle, president of Phillips Investment Resources, for their belief in our cause and support of our development. Without you I would still be e-mailing stock ideas to my e-mail list late at night.

A very significant debt of gratitude goes to Darlene March (a.k.a. "The Ferret"), whose unconquerable spirit and moxy launched me into the world of financial television and radio. From humble beginnings, we now reach hundreds of thousands of homes each month thanks to the work of Darlene and the ever-expanding reach of the Fox News Channel. Special thanks as well go to the Fox News Channel business team, especially the lovely and talented Brenda Buttner for "discovering" me, Neil Cavuto and Roger Ailes for taking a risk on an unknown investment analyst, and Gary Schreier, the producer extraordinaire who makes all of us on *Bulls & Bears* look so good each week.

Every day I learn something new in the world of investing in stocks for a living, and I thank Bryan Perry, Katy Atkinson, and all the ChangeWave Capital Management team for helping me run our mutual fund and hedge fund services so smoothly that I can devote time to writing.

On a more personal note, I thank the Desperados, my Southern California crew of family and friends, and the Provine Gang, whose friendship I miss terribly during weekends of writing and working but whose support has always been a blessing. Looking forward to adventures with friends makes all the work less onerous.

Finally, much thanks and love to my wife, Marjorie, for cheerfully supporting me on this project and in the pursuit of the ChangeWave dream as well. Many late nights and busted weekends go into a book, and I am eternally grateful for her continued faith and love throughout.

PREFACE

Why Do Investors Need ChangeWave 2.0?

The original *ChangeWave Investing* book was published in June 1999. Why a new version so soon after the original?

Because just about everything about ChangeWave Investing has changed or been updated. As we planned it would, I might add.

Everything *except* our core philosophy of using high magnitudes of change to help everyday investors like you find the most lucrative opportunities for investment profits independent of Wall Street's conflict-ridden analyst system.

Our goal, as always, is to teach you how to find the *genuinely* transformational economic, technological, regulatory, and/or strategic shifts in an industry or company we call *ChangeQuakes.* These turn into high-octane, irreversible waves of growth we call *ChangeWaves.* Finding and analyzing great magnitudes of change is still the most reliable "radar system" for finding monster growth stocks we know.

But even as ChangeWave investors were successfully using our simple buy-and-sell approach to ride the wealth-building waves of creative destruction and corporate self-renewal, problems were surfacing elsewhere. Congress, for the first time in our history, held hearings in June 2001 on the dysfunctional practices of stock pushers masquerading as "securities analysts."

What Congress wanted to know was why only 1% of analyst recommendations were "sell" at the same time that American investors were losing roughly $4 trillion of newly created wealth. Not surprisingly to our ChangeWave investment community, the real meaning of the unspoken Wall Street motto, "Whose bread I eat, his song I sing," was finally made clear to the rest of the country. Loyalty on Wall Street has always been bestowed upon whoever paid the most. It always will be.

The meltdown of technology and Internet stock prices in 2000–2001 seems to have helped much of the general investing public to realize that, if they were going to reach their investment goals, they couldn't rely on

Wall Street's investment advice. As Rep. Richard H. Baker, chairman of the House Financial Services Committee, said in his opening statement, "The foundation of the free-market system is the free flow of straightforward, unbiased information. And I must say I am deeply troubled by evidence of Wall Street's erosion of the bedrock of ethical conduct." He went on to quote from a Harvard and Wharton Business School study that stated, "Our evidence suggests that the coexistence of brokerage services and underwriting services in the same institution leads sell-side analysts to compromise their responsibility to brokerage clients in order to attract underwriting business."

As Benjamin Cole, a financial journalist and author, testified before the committee, "What the general investing public doesn't realize yet is that Wall Street research has become hopelessly corrupt."

But in reality it's not fair to pile on the sell-side analysts. They are only doing their job. The point is their job was *never* to deliver unbiased industry and company analysis to help advise individual investors.

Their job is to help institutional investors to take a pulse, see what others are thinking, and then decide which side of the story they belive in. Period. ChangeWave Investing is an alternative to the Wall Street analyst system. And it has come just in time. As highly regarded Wall Street analyst Andy Kessler states in the *Wall Street Journal,* July 2001, "Say good-bye to analysts. The S.E.C.'s regulation regarding full disclosure has already wiped out most of their value. Money managers do their own work, and the public will have to as well. With the democratization of the financial markets, we are *all* analysts now." Well, if we are all analysts now, consider this book your first training guide.

Wall Street and its participants are in the game for one reason—to make *themselves* rich. If nothing else, I hope the ideas we first brought forward in our ChangeWave approach have proved the concept that "independent analyst" is at best an oxymoron.

How does ChangeWave Investing help the individual investor remove himself or herself from the Wall Street analyst quagmire? Simply put, ChangeWave Investing offers investors a few simple rules to accurately analyze and profitably "ride" wealth-building waves of transformational change—usually before the analysts have even recognized them. Simpler yet: ChangeWave Investing is about you putting your investment capital on the winning side of change by learning how *not* to be dependent on Wall Street research. Perhaps more exciting, thousands of like-minded ChangeWave investors have banded together to share their ChangeWave discoveries, making our alternative approach to investing all the more attractive to time-constrained investors.

CHANGEWAVE IS STILL ABOUT CHANGE

Why our fixation on change? Because irreversible, noncyclical change (or what is known on Wall Street as "secular" change), more than any other economic power, creates the opportunity for profit. And, as the great Internet stock bubble so painfully retaught investors, the only thing that creates true economic value is profitability. Thus, a noncyclical change creates the opportunity for the creation of *massive* profitability—which in turn drives an equally powerful creation and destruction of economic value and wealth.

In short: If you want to find really big monster stocks, you first have to be able to find the monster transformations within the economy *before* everyone else catches on—*before* Wall Street starts pumping up their "new" latest and greatest investment banking client.

The "before everyone else" part sounds like a tall order. But take heart. The velocity of change in the business world has continued to accelerate in recent years. As the renowned technology guru and futurist Ray Kurzweil points out in an April 2001 edition of *Talk* magazine, "Progress is becoming so fast that it will confound our ability to follow it."

In fact, if you're feeling overwhelmed by the rate and magnitude of change in our world today, I have bad news: It's speeding up. According to Kurzweil, "While most forecasters use linear models to predict the future, the fact is our rate of progress now doubles every *decade*—which makes our rate of change exponential."

Exponential rates of change? History proves Kurzweil out. The nineteenth century saw more technological change than the nine centuries preceding it. In the first twenty years of the twentieth century, we witnessed more advancement than we did in the nineteenth century. Change over the past decade dwarfs the rate of change of even thirty years ago. We expect to see a century of progress over the next twenty years. In a linearly changing world, this amount of change, according to Kurzweil, would take 200 centuries.

Of course, this explosion in transformational change is driven by the explosion in Internet communications and information technology. Despite the collapse of Internet companies, the Internet itself continues to grow at blinding speed, transforming traditional companies in myriad ways. This information-transfer-on-steroids feeds on itself and thus accelerates the pace of change.

But as unsettling as the ever-increasing rate of change may be to your senses, exponential rates of change mean equally high rates of wealth creation. (There had to be *some* benefit to mind-numbing rates of change, right?)

The good news is that ever-increasing rates of transformational change mean ever-increasing opportunities for you to get rich investing.

In Chapters 5 to 10, we'll teach you the basics of becoming a proficient and profitable "change analyst." In my opinion, developing your skills as a change analyst—that is, accurately analyzing change opportunities in the economy in terms of their magnitude and impact, and understanding who the primary beneficiary of such change is—is the most important investing skill you can develop.

Perhaps the best example of how exponential vs. linear rates of change affects our lives is to quickly look at how the world and our investment tactics have changed since we published *ChangeWave Investing* in June 1999. Let's start with the concept we fought so hard for years to validate: the emergence of a new phase of economic growth.

THE NEW ECONOMY BECAME THE REAL ECONOMY

What New Economy? There is no "New Economy," as some called the post-1995 economic age started by the emergence of an ultracompetitive/ultraproductive global marketplace based on a common standard method of communication (i.e., the Internet). How do we know? Alan Greenspan told us.

Years ago we had a daily argument with economists, investment professionals, and portfolio managers about the economic, industrial, and social ramifications brought about by the Internet and its single unifying system for data/voice/video/audio communications. We used the term *New Economy* as a linguistic weapon in our defense of our assertion that we had entered an era with a new engine of economic growth.

But many took this concept way too far. We don't have a New Economy per se. We simply have the Real Economy. But because of massive changes in its political, technological, and communication fabric, it really is different.

Today our economy is really *more competitive, more global,* really *innovation-based,* really *more productive,* and really *faster-changing.*

What is *new* about the Real Economy is that it is an irreversible conversion to a new economic productivity infrastructure—that is, the Internet.

High-speed and broadband Internet Protocol–based computing and communicating is well on its way to becoming the standard and primary productivity tool for virtually every industry of the twenty-first century. Andy Grove of Intel fame predicts that by 2005, 100% of small to midsize companies will have "Webified" their businesses.

Why should investors care? Because, as with all new economic engines of past economic eras (steam power, electricity, the semiconductor), higher economic productivity brings with it higher levels of prosperity and quality of life for all those who learn to use this new, vastly powerful economic tool.

While the New Economy morphed into the Real Economy, the building blocks *are* different. Today's most valuable and value-creating assets are minds and intellectual properties rather than machines and real-estate properties. Our raw materials are often bits of data rather than atoms. Our freight trains are more likely to be packets of light racing down optical cables rather than cars on railroad tracks.

For investors, the most important facet to this latest version of the Real Economy is its improved fundamental capability to sustain *inflation-resistant growth.* This most current industrial revolution, built on the new exponentially faster and broader-based Internet Protocol (or IP) productivity platform, has the ability to grow faster with less inflationary risk than any economy of the past.

Since inflation is kryptonite to stock valuations, inflation-resistant growth is simply the best possible environment for your money to grow rapidly into real wealth via stocks.

In Chapter 2, I'll describe the new fundamental power behind the enormous potential for new wealth creation over the next decade. We'll discuss Alan Greenspan's revelations about the "New Economy" and how one of the most powerful ChangeQuakes and ChangeWaves of the twentieth century continues to gain momentum and strength today.

But the Real Economy we live in is as vulnerable to the ups and downs of the business cycle as always, as the capital spending recession of 2000–2001 taught us.

History has proved that, no matter how powerful the technology, it will never be a match for the forces that periodically overwhelm the economy: rising interest rates, restrictive monetary policy, falling profits, shrinking consumer demand, plunging stock prices, too much debt, frightened lenders, and money-wasting government spending.

The business cycle is alive, and you had better have an investment strategy that can deal with it. In Chapter 14, I'll show you how.

CORPORATE AMERICA CHANGED

In the last year, corporate America finally got it: The New Economy was no more about technology than the Gold Rush was about shovels. Technology does not create change, it creates opportunities—in this case, for higher fundamental levels of productivity and lower costs of doing business. But these changes take time. For example, the studies of Stanford University professor Paul David found that while electricity was widely deployed in 1890 the effects did not show up in a meaningful way until the 1920s. Until electricity was matched with miniature electrical motors, the opportunity of fundamental change from electrical power was not realized.

The initial change in corporate America came as information technology shifted from an expense or cost center on the corporate ledger to a profit-making/savings-protecting center. To most businesses the ability to harness information technology became a strategic and revenue-positive pillar of the modern company. Information technology rose to more than 50% of capital spending budgets—on its way to 70% by 2010, according to some estimates.

These revelations occurred about the same time that another New Economy myth was being burst.

THE DOT-COM BUBBLE

The late, great economist Joseph Schumpeter, who coined the concept and phrase "creative destruction," never lived to see his thesis proved deadly accurate. This uniquely capitalistic phenomenon of industrial construction and destruction hit the Internet-based business like a tornado in 1998–2000. In the year 2001, most dot-com companies folded like a mobile home in a class five twister.

I say good riddance. And hurrah, because it means capitalism works! The 15 minutes of fame for dot-com companies that created no innovative new value for people (and thus no profitability/economic value for those companies) confused investors about the bigger issue at hand. That issue is the latest reconstruction of our economy launched by the Internet "Big Bang." In Chapter 7, we'll make sure *you* don't confuse real businesses for pretend businesses.

The Darwinian destruction of weak businesses (and their stock prices) was swift and brutal—and completely necessary to complete the creative destruction cycle. And to prove the basic laws of technology business valuation—the Law of Disproportionate Reward (i.e., the propensity for 90% of market value in technology markets to go to 10% of the participants) is alive and well. We'll make sure you are well versed in both in Chapter 12.

REACTING TO CHANGE BY CHANGING OUR PORTFOLIO

With our selling discipline, we sold pretty much all of our stocks since we published *ChangeWave Investing.* "Kicking off" peaking ChangeWaves is as much a part of ChangeWave Investing as riding them—any surfer will tell you that. As so many investors learned, waiting for Wall Street to provide sell guidance on a stock they once suggested buying is a very expensive exercise in futility.

That investors make a profit investing in stocks only when they *sell* them is a lesson many investors have learned the hard way since June 2000.

We learned to smooth out our portfolio performance by adding a whole different category of industries and stocks to our growth investing approach—we call these industries and stocks "ballast growth." You'll learn how they can safeguard your investment profits in Chapter 9.

Riding the fastest-growing ChangeWaves in our economy by investing in emerging industry growth stocks was intended to be only a part of a well-balanced portfolio. Most investors thought a well-balanced portfolio was owning twenty-five tech stocks instead of one hundred. I've clarified and explained how to balance out a portfolio of aggressive- and speculative-growth stocks with lower-volatility growth stocks from ballast-growth industries. These stocks are still growing at 25%-plus growth rates, but they are not in the top 1% of all industrial growth rates like our emerging ChangeWave industries. However, these ballast-growth markets are huge ($10 billion-plus) and strongly growing.

More important, these economically less sensitive ChangeWaves, such as independent power production, health care services, and water infrastructure engineering, smooth out the ups and downs of your overall ChangeWave growth stock portfolio. They serve literally as ballast during the rough seas of market corrections and the predictable bear market we encounter every four years or so.

Our ballast-growth holdings proved particularly valuable when . . .

THE GREAT TECHNOLOGY
1995–2000 BULL MARKET ENDED

Economist John Maynard Keynes once said, "Investment is an activity of forecasting the yield on assets over the life of the asset; . . . speculation is the activity of forecasting the psychology of the market."

To ChangeWave investors, the most significant change from the original investment strategies offered in ChangeWave Investing was the collapse of the speculative bubble that exploded the value of our Nasdaq-listed ChangeWave stocks. Early on in the decline that we foresaw, we developed new and improved selling strategies for ChangeWave investors to protect their capital and make profitable investments within an environment of bear market pessimism.

More important, we added a vital new leg to our overall growth investing strategy.

THE GROWTH APPROPRIATE TO
THE BUSINESS CYCLE STRATEGY

Bear markets come and go, and always will, because we have a boom-to-bust, business-cycle-based economy. The biggest fallacy of the 1999–2000 Nasdaq stock bubble was that the industrial age economic cycle of gross domestic product (GDP) expansion, peaking, contracting, bottoming/troughing, and reexpanding had gone the way of the dodo bird. Boy, was that an expensive lesson!

The second-biggest myth slain by the big bad bear of 2000–2001 was the idea that information technology industries were not cyclical industries dependent on an expanding economy to sustain their extraordinarily high growth rates. The one-two-three punch of explosion of demand from telecom deregulation in 1996, the ephemeral Y2K panic, and the Internet mania created the illusion that enormous rates of information technology spending had become business cycle *independent.*

Wrong!

Our "Growth Appropriate to the Business Cycle," or GAB, strategy served us well in the bear market of 2000–2001. You'll learn in Chapter 13 how ChangeWave Investing can preserve and grow your investment capital in bear as well as bull markets.

ChangeWave investors use bear markets to get the lowest cost basis possible in the very strongest leaders of most powerful next-generation ChangeWaves. But our GAB strategy makes sure you have the buying power required to cash in on the inevitable break in pessimism that follows these periods of gloomy, "glass-half-empty" bear markets.

ChangeWave Investing 2.0 prepares you for another phenomenon I did not cover in my first book—what we call the Momentum Zone. Our selling discipline has evolved to help ChangeWave investors protect and yet maximize profits when one of their fundamentally great stocks gets sucked up into the typhoon of momentum—investors buying or selling the stock simply because it's going up or down. We teach you how to miss the inevitable crash of these momentum waves in Chapter 11.

In Chapter 9, I introduce the idea of "MarketQuakes," or radical shifts in the macroeconomic and capital markets world that are deadly accurate in projecting the expansion, transition, and contraction phases of the business cycle. In less than 10 minutes a month, ChangeWave investors can learn how to use these MarketQuakes to shift their Growth Appropriate to the Business Cycle portfolio balance between aggressive/speculative growth and ballast growth in order to avoid the capital killing aspects of prolonged bear markets on your money.

Waiting for Wall Street economists to forecast an economic downturn is the second-longest wait an investor will ever experience. (The longest wait, of course, is for a sell signal.) Learning how to safeguard your growth stocks against a coming bear market storm is another critical tool investors need to become "rich and analyst free."

CHANGEWAVE INVESTING: A MONEY MANAGEMENT STRATEGY

Since the original book was written, I have taken the same strategies and tactics I write about here and have used them to manage millions of dollars in both private and public investment funds. The lessons I learn every day have helped to refine aspects of our strategy discussed here in the book and on our ChangeWave.com Web site.

Believe me: There is nothing like making multimillion-dollar decisions every day to shake down an investment strategy into its simplest and most effective form.

Think of *ChangeWave Investing 2.0* as our "manifesto" and guidebook on how to become rich and analyst free—how to become a truly independent investor. I believe more strongly than ever that the odds of building true wealth through stocks are exponentially higher for investors who are not dependent or captive to Wall Street for their buy, hold, and sell information.

Investing can be broken into two distinct parts: stock-picking strategy and portfolio-management tactics. One without the other, over time, results in mediocre investment results. You and I will start with the basic concepts and strategies necessary for you to become a first-class "change analyst," which is crucial to your success in monster-stock hunting. I then teach you the basics of tactical, click-by-click, aggressive-growth portfolio management, ChangeWave style.

Through the efforts of literally tens of thousands of ChangeWave investors, ChangeWave Investing has become a viable alternative to the traditional Wall Street investment research complex. I invite you to become part of our solution to the analyst problem by helping us rewrite the rules of investing—in your favor! Remember, the goal of ChangeWave Investing is to help *you* get rich. When you succeed, we succeed, too.

Welcome to the Wave!

CHANGEWAVE INVESTING 2.0

PART ONE

The Keys to the Growth Stock World: Becoming a Change Expert

CHAPTER ONE

What Is ChangeWave Investing?

ChangeWave Investing is a philosophy, a growth-stock-picking strategy, and portfolio-management system rolled into one. The basic philosophy is simple: I believe the greatest power driving the future appreciation or depreciation of business value (in other words, future amount of profitability) is transformational change.

That means incidences of transformational change at the industry or corporate level are the most accurate leading indicators of future stock appreciation.

I've found from my years of research into the dynamics of change and stock prices that transformational change, and how a company does or does not embrace and leverage it—more than any other business or analysis factor—determines the profitability, and thus the appreciation potential, of a company. Stock market bubbles notwithstanding, my research says that, in today's world, creating and managing transformational change and innovation *is* the strategy of building the economic value of a business—everything else is just tactics.

The primary takeaway from the entire book is this: If you are lucky enough to have found genuine transformational change beginning to explode within an industry or company, you've found a genuine investment opportunity—an investment opportunity that just could change your financial life forever.

Because when you find genuinely transformational change, you find big winners and big losers. What the ChangeWave strategy helps you do is:

* Find the highest-magnitude (read: "most profitable") transformational changes occurring within industries and companies
* Locate the sweet spots of investment opportunity (read: "best-performing market spaces") within these waves of transformation we call ChangeWaves
* Put your money on the winning stocks within these hot market spaces and keep it away from the losers, the victims of transformation change

In other words, ChangeWave Investing helps you get "luckier" than most investors will ever be.

We use a set of simple rules to search for and analyze the magnitude of changes occurring in our economy to gain a relative context. This set of rules acts like a "change analysis prism" to determine the biggest potential winners and losers in our perpetually changing world.

In a nutshell, I describe the strategy as learning how to analyze the dynamics of rapid, structural transformational change—that is, "investable change"—through an imaginary lens or prism composed of the unchanging laws or elements of human behavior.

In ChangeWave Investing, we use fixed laws of human behavior to put the blurry snapshots of a rapidly changing world into focus. When you apply the virtually never-changing laws of human behavior to a rapidly or radically changing business situation, repeatable patterns emerge that can significantly enhance your investment returns.

This lens or analytical prism acts as radar does for a pilot landing in a blur of fog. Rapid rates of change create a foglike condition that makes it very difficult for most investors, and indeed the financial community, to get their bearings. Our prism helps us see through the fog and discover the value hidden to most investors.

Perhaps Terry Matthews, self-made multibillionaire in telecom equipment, defined the ChangeWave Investing strategy best in an interview with *Forbes* magazine. "You put yourself out on a board," he said. "A lot of waves come in, but only about one wave in ten is a big motherin' wave that will give you a great ride. That's the only wave I want to catch."

While I agree with Mr. Matthews wholeheartedly, I'd add one thought: While he is referring to the great waves of creative destruction in technology (where huge technological leaps lead telecom companies to rip out billions of dollars of old gear and replace it with billions of dollars of new gear), there are great waves of new spending and huge waves of increased profits in *all* types of industries.

Transformational change is an equal-opportunity wealth builder and destroyer. It is not just about tech stocks.

YOU AS MASTER CHANGE ANALYST

The focus of *ChangeWave Investing 2.0* is to show you how to become a successful change analyst. When you become one, you'll be able to apply your knowledge to making more money in your stock portfolio than you have ever made before.

What you actually become good at is separating *true* investable change from its lower-magnitude, less-profitable incremental change. (This skill is also quite beneficial in helping you to improve your business and career decisions, too.)

The key advantage ChangeWave investors hold is developing high levels of confidence in reading and reacting to rapidly transforming industries and companies a little *earlier* and a little *better* than everyone else does. Our ChangeWave portfolio management strategies also help you hold on to these winners during market turbulence when others sell prematurely.

YOUR EDGE ON THE MARKET

In investing, you need only a little edge to outperform the market as a whole. The effectiveness of the ChangeWave Investing strategy in every-day buying and selling of stocks points to the impact of the edge we offer.

How effective? Well, the application of the strategy and buy/sell/hold tactics has resulted in buying and selling stocks that have delivered on average 75%-a-year growth in our model portfolio since 1995. Including the Nasdaq crash of 2000–2001.

We'll start with the basic concepts and strategies necessary for you to become a first-class "change analyst," which is crucial to your success in monster-stock hunting. Then we'll get into the blocking and tackling of Growth Appropriate to the Business Cycle portfolio management, ChangeWave style.

But before we get to the strategy and tactics, given the crazy stock market of the twenty-first century so far, perhaps we should start with why you should bother investing in growth stocks in the first place.

CHAPTER TWO

The Case for Growth Investing in the Early Twenty-First Century

As I said in the introduction, we stand at a moment in time where a century of progress and transformational change will occur before our eyes in just the next twenty years.

If you believe our basic premise that the magnitude of investment opportunity you face is a direct function of the magnitude of transformational change you find, you may be ready to go directly to Chapter 5.

But many investors today are still fighting the New Economy/Old Economy fight while they lick their deep wounds from the last bear market. Many investors are caught up in dismissing the latest new leg of the modern industrialism as a one-time aberration—a fluke of economics, or a one-time-only event.

These misguided souls are bound to miss the big picture and the immense profits ahead. I don't want you to be one of them.

THE DAY THE NEW ECONOMY
WAS BORN AND DIED

When I wrote *ChangeWave Investing* two years ago, we were still fighting the "New Economy versus Old Economy" fight. What happened in twenty-four months? How did a formerly difficult-to-win argument become a non-argument?

The argument died the day that Alan Greenspan finally understood what the New Economy really was about.

I can even name the flash point: October 19, 2000, Greenspan's speech at the Cato Institute in Washington. No cameras, no press. It was the moment when I knew deep in my heart we were not in Kansas anymore. Said Greenspan:

> By now, the story of the boom in information technology is well-known, and nearly everyone perceives that the resulting more rapid growth of labor productivity is at least partly enduring. . . . Some who question the economic implications of the spread of innovation and the step up in productivity growth hypothesize that the gains are largely confined to the so-called New Economy, with little effect on efficiency in the Old Economy.
>
> But this notion fails to capture the dynamics of the marketplace. . . . [There is] little of a truly Old Economy left. Virtually every part of our economic structure is, to a greater or lesser extent, affected by the newer innovations . . . almost all parts of our economy have shared to some extent in the benefits of this wave of innovation.

Although these comments received virtually no media coverage (the press focused primarily on his remarks to Cato concerning oil prices), their implications for what I have called the Real Economy argument were crucial. From that evening on, it became clear that without compelling evidence convincing him otherwise, Mr. Greenspan was finally persuaded that sustainable productivity gains are capable of supporting GDP growth rates well in excess of 4%—throughout our economy, Old and New combined.

He went on to support this thesis in classic Greenspan-speak:

[Economic models] are a major simplification of the many forces that govern the functioning of our system at any point in time. . . . Obviously, to the extent that these constructs . . . fail to capture critical factors driving economic expansion or contraction, conclusions drawn from their application will be off the mark.

With the virtually unprecedented surge in innovation that we have experienced . . . many of the economic relationships embodied in past models no longer project outcomes that mirror the newer realities.

When confronted with a period of structural change, our policy actions must be based on identifying emerging trends from surprises and anomalies in the data, and then carefully drawing their implications. It would be folly to cling to an antiquated model in the face of contradictory information.

What Greenspan meant was that when the Internet and information technology—the ultimate deflationary tools—are embedded in the corporate world, inflation over the long term will be tamed and productivity will be structurally improved for the better. Forever.

What's important to realize is that we are, as ZDNet editor-in-chief Dan Farber likes to say, merely in the "cave-drawing" period of the next industrial revolutionary phase. In the second phase of this economic revolution, we are now seeing the emergence of what I call the "EverNet," where literally billions of digital devices—from PCs to cellular phones—become connected to an increasingly powerful high-speed-broadband, multiple-format Web.

Legendary tech investor Roger McNamee perhaps says it best: "Everything that is interesting in the marketplace today derives from the transition to real-time computing."

Just the inflation and productivity implications of an economy-wide transition to 24/7 real-time business management itself is incredibly bullish for equity investing over the long term. But it gets much better.

WE HAVE NOT YET FIGURED OUT
HOW PRODUCTIVE WE REALLY ARE

Our institutions, the U.S. government, and most economists don't yet have a clue about how to measure the real impact of a globally wired, real-time EverNet world on our economic productivity.

A great example of this reality gap came October 28, 1999, when the federal Bureau of Economic Analysis (BEA) decided to change the accounting rules on the purchase of software. The BEA has admittedly undercounted the value of software for years by treating it as a raw material to be used in the production of other goods and services. By changing the depreciable life of software from an immediate expense to a depreciable asset, expensed over its useful life, the BEA finally recognized that the useful life of software is longer than the minute it is first used. This one move *significantly* recast the measurement of economic productivity for the past twenty years.

Now, I don't want to go off on a Dennis Miller rant here, but just wait until twenty years from now, when the "experts" abandon their 500-year-old accounting system designed to count bales of hay and widgets. They will go back and revise the productivity rates and reportable earnings of intellectual-asset- or knowledge-asset-based companies by 15% to 25% or more to the positive.

We'll get a glimpse of this phenomenon when the rules for amortization of goodwill (i.e., the amount paid for a company in excess of its tangible book value) change July 1, 2001.

Harvard accounting professor Robert Kaplan says in the February 2000 issue of *CFO* magazine: "Today, the long-term success of organizations comes from their knowledge-based assets—customer relationships; innovative products and services; operationally excellent processes; the skills, capabilities and motivation of their people; and their databases and information systems. Physical assets may be important, but they are unlikely to be as effective a competitive weapon as intangible knowledge assets."

Perhaps Baruch Leve, professor of accounting at UC Berkeley and the Stern School at NYU, best critiques the inadequacy of ancient accounting practices to capture a clear picture of corporate value in what I have begun to call our emerging "Techonomy." (I define *techonomy* as an economy where a majority of its gross domestic product comes from industries primarily addressing the creation, transportation, computing, viewing or utilization of bits of *data* instead of *physical products.*) Says Leve: "Transactions are no longer the basis for much of the value created in today's economy. And therefore traditional accounting systems are at a loss to capture much of what goes on. For example, when a drug passes a key clinical test, or a software program is successfully beta-tested, great value is created without any transaction taking place. There's no accounting event because no money changes hands."

Highly respected Philadelphia Federal Reserve Bank economist Leonard Nakamura has pioneered this shift in thinking. To paraphrase Mr. Nakamura, one day we will "learn" that what we really should have been doing all along is capitalizing the investments companies make in intangible assets, instead of immediately expensing their development costs and deducting the expense from current earnings. On the day we begin to do that, everyone will recognize that intellectual-property-based companies have for decades financially outperformed their physical-asset-based cousins by a mind-blowing order-of-magnitude difference.

But please don't wait until then.

Because with the EverNet becoming the world's common platform for communication and productivity, we have clearly entered a new age of value creation. Which means . . .

THE BEST WEALTH-BUILDING OPPORTUNITIES ARE YET TO COME

I am personally convinced that you and I have before us, over the next decade, the greatest long-term investment opportunity of any generation in history.

I come to this conclusion simply because we are so early in the next great wealth-creation shift in human history. Since around 1995, the basis of wealth creation (i.e., how value is uniquely created for customers and thus wealth-creating profits generated for those who provide that value) has shifted irreversibly. It has shifted from the last great value-creation paradigm of manufacturing and transportation of goods, to value and wealth creation primarily made by information, knowledge, and connectivity values added to basic services and products (i.e., leveraging the EverNet).

When James Watt perfected the steam engine in 1769, the basis for both value creation (i.e., how you add economic value to raw materials) and wealth creation shifted irreversibly. *It shifted from the ownership of land, to manufacturing and transportation,* both made possible by the steam engine, and later the development of the internal combustion engine and the electric motor in the 1870s. As leading growth fund portfolio manager Robert Loest, Ph.D., CFA, points out, "For the first time in history, one could buy a measly acre of land, put a manufacturing facility on it, and make physical goods in large numbers and higher quality. This created value *totally independent of the ownership of land!* One could also build a steamship, and ship enormously more goods and types of goods, including fresh produce, in a fraction of the time required by sailing ships. This expanded international trade and wealth, and created enormous value, all without the ownership of land. Amazing."

Like the early investors who profited greatly from the last great shift from an agrarian economy to an industrial economy, you and I are fortunate to be alive and investing at the dawn of this new and extraordinary wealth-creation cycle.

Even better, history shows us that a disproportionate amount of new wealth is created in the beginning stages of these rare economic transformations.

WHAT'S NEW ABOUT WEALTH BUILDING TODAY?

The key to building wealth today is substituting knowledge and information for physical assets. Most new wealth in our economy is being created by applying and leveraging rich information and creative brainpower. Cisco or Intel or Microsoft consumes few scarce resources making products. They mostly consume ever-expandable resources, such as ideas, computer power, and real-time customer feedback.

Consider the great paradox of the wealth creation: Bill Gates, the king of this new digital knowledge economy, owns virtually no land, gold, or industrial processes. The book value (i.e., tangible financial and physical assets) of Microsoft is near $49 billion, yet the market value is near $380 billion as of this writing.

How does one explain this incredible wealth-creation divergence? Is it an anomaly?

How does one account for the trillions of dollars of market valuation of thousands of companies, driven primarily by ideas and brain-powered "knowledge capital," which enjoy market values 100 to 1,000 times their book or physical asset value?

The answer comes from a quick and painless economics lesson, one that Tom Petzinger Jr. discussed recently in the *Wall Street Journal.* In his insightful analysis, he asks us to think of an economy as the sum of every action people take to provide themselves and others *more* with *less.* In one way or another, wealth-creating innovations have always substituted knowledge or capital for energy, materials, or labor.

The introduction of the three-field system (a form of crop rotation) in medieval Europe increased agricultural output as sharply as broadband datacom is contributing to communication today. In the nineteenth century, the steam engine replaced human and animal labor with mechanical energy. Ever since the invention of the wheel, this process of doing more with fewer resources has been the source of wealth creation. It always will be.

What this massive transition in value creation means to investors is simple. There are massive amounts of new profits and new wealth being made in front of your eyes. If you are looking to grow your wealth radically, you need to have radically transforming marketplaces.

But there are bigger forces at work here that make you and me even more fortunate.

CREATIVE DESTRUCTION IS DRIVING OUR ECONOMY

This great wealth- and value-creation shift in which we are living is driven by a new chapter or era in the age of industrialism. Change expert Dr. Peter Bishop of the University of Houston, in his article "The Waves of Creative Destruction," helps explain this phenomenon.

According to Dr. Bishop:

> The great economist Joseph Schumpeter saw the progress of industrialism as a series of stages, each powered by one or more lead technologies. A lead technology is one that is so much more productive than what it replaces that it offers a significant boost to the productivity of the overall economy. Not only do the industries directly involved with the invention and application of the lead technology benefit, but the whole economy grows because of the productivity realized.
>
> In the end, every organization must adopt this new, highly productive technology in order to match the productivity of its competitors or face extinction. The waves are creative—they create new things; but they are also destructive—they eventually require everyone to abandon old practices and ways of doing business.

The first "lead technology" of the industrial age was the textile industry centered in Britain in the eighteenth and early nineteenth centuries. The application of the power loom, the spinning jenny, and the cotton gin to the handcrafted business of turning cotton and wool into cloth and apparel was nothing short of a revolution. The technology (in this case, the machines) could do in minutes what it took hours to accomplish by hand—and do it better, without sleep and twenty-four hours a day if needed. The amazing productivity boost fueled the trade routes of the British empire for decades and gave industrialism its first leg of growth. The increase in the profits realized from these activities was staggering.

According to Dr. Bishop, the first lead technology to transform the United States was the railroad after the Civil War (powered by the steam engine, of course). An almost exclusive agricultural nation at the time, the United States applied the railroad line like no other nation of the era. Rail lines (built from the proceeds of stock sold during the great railroad stock bull market, I might add) transformed the nation from a coastal to a continental power. The trains carried natural resources and goods for pennies on the dollar compared to the horse-drawn wagons of old. Not only was this the basis for agriculture, mining, and timber, but it also established the mail-order business and telegraph. Sears, Roebuck and Montgomery Ward both began in Chicago because that was where the rails converged and a midwest location was perfect for a distribution center.

How powerful are these lead-technology transformations? Dr. Bishop tells the story of how Jay Gould, a leading railroad magnate of his day, came to Jefferson, Texas, with an offer to put a railhead in their fair city. The city fathers turned him down. Instead, Gould settled on his second choice—a small, insignificant town named Dallas. Today, Jefferson is a quaint bedroom community, and Dallas is one of the largest cities in the United States.

Additional waves of creative destruction resulted from the application of electricity, steel, and finally oil to the economic landscape of the late nineteenth and early twentieth centuries.

All these ex–lead technologies are with us today. But they play a small part in the next wave or leap in productivity: perpetual information and knowledge connectivity. Those lead technologies are the microprocessor and dense wave multiplexing photonics carrying data on waves of light down fiber-optic cable.

Make no mistake, the transformation of our mass-production, geographically restricted, physical-asset-based economy to a digitally internetworked, brain-powered, intangible-asset-based economy represents as revolutionary a lead technology as any of the past waves of creative destruction in industrialism.

"Virtually unimaginable a half century ago," says Alan Greenspan, "was the extent to which concepts and ideas would substitute for physical resources and human brawn in the production of goods and services."

Traditional economics saw wealth (and profits) flowing primarily from an organization's land, capital, labor, and entrepreneurship. Land, and then capital, were seen as the scarcest resources. Labor was abundant, used by owners of land and capital to exploit their resources.

Today, the majority of new wealth flows from new profits derived from patented, trademarked, copyrighted, or proprietary algorithms, software, formulas, business processes, brands—that is, information and ideas. That's all exploited, in the true sense of the word, by its owners to add value to basic materials and services. What is scarcest in our technology-driven world is universal agreement on common technology protocols and standards.

It is the combined effect of the new lead technologies of the twenty-first century, culminating in what I call the EverNet, that creates the most bullish scenario of all for investors. . . .

CHAPTER THREE

The Emerging American "Techonomy"

The long-term wave of infotech-based GDP growth is quickly changing the fundamental nature of our economy *massively* . . . for the better.

Up to 40% of U.S. GDP growth over the last few years has come from infotech-related industries, services, and natural resource spending. This number is all the more compelling in that infotech's share of our entire GDP is less than 15%—for now.

Even without the overspending in infotech and telecom technologies during the 1996–2000 tech-spending orgy, corporate capital expenditures budgets continue to average over 50% on information technology in 2001. And according to the infotech research group Gartner, this figure will grow to 70% by 2010.

The key premise of our bullish outlook for continued economic growth and significantly higher future equity valuations comes from the irreversibly higher trajectory of the infotech ecosystem's growth versus non-infotech industrial growth over the next decade. The wide disparity between the growth rate of the information technology gross domestic product and the output of the Old Economy puts the United States on track to becoming what I call the world's first "Techonomy." That means an economy where more than 50% of GDP spending comes from industries within the information technology ecosystem of enabling natural resources, power systems, technology, and services.

The only question is "How long is this historic transition going to take?"

THE NEW TECHONOMY: 2010 OR 2020?

I define the Techonomy ecosystem as the entire food chain of spending from the basic natural resources to the products and services required to create, transport, secure, store, compute, and render digital bits of data for commercial or personal use throughout the economy.

Do the Techonomy math. The best case, Scenario No. 1, estimates GDP growth rates of Techonomy-related capital, wage, and consumption spending in the United States to revert to 18% per year throughout the next decade, *after* the economy recovers from the infotech/ telecom spending bubble. Non-Techonomy industries (i.e., Old Economy or non-infotech products and services) are projected to grow by about 2%.

At these disparate growth rates, the U.S. economy will cross over to an economy where more than 50% of our GDP spending will go to Techonomy products, services, or related enabling resources by 2008. The economic reality of business in the twenty-first century is irrefutable: Companies desiring to build or maintain competitive advantages and attractive profit margins have no choice. They have to replace profit-robbing overhead (read: low-valued staff) with many forms of information and communications technology.

Scenario No. 2 (the most likely case) estimates Techonomy GDP growth rates to average only 9% a year, extending the conversion process through 2020.

In either scenario, the implication of this irreversible transition are both startling and profoundly bullish for stock market investors.

Scenario No. 1

Year	Infotech Ecosystem GDP (%)	Non-Techonomy GDP (%)
2000	**24.4**	**75.6**
2001	27.3	72.7
2002	30.5	69.5
2003	33.9	66.1
2004	37.5	62.5
2005	41.3	58.7
2006	45.5	54.5
2007	49.3	50.7
2008	**53.3**	**46.7**

When you invest in stocks, you are making a bet on the future. And in the United States, a Techonomy *is* the future.

Strategic Techonomic Resource: Energy

The creation of data bits starts with its fundamental energy resource: natural gas and coal. Natural gas has become the key natural resource needed for the creation of electricity. The *Wall Street Journal* reports that "90% of the new electrical power generation facilities under construction are powered by natural gas." Sixteen percent of U.S. electricity is generated from gas-powered turbines—and the percentage is growing quickly. Yet today more than 50% of electrical power comes from coal-fired generators, which makes coal the most basic energy resource of the emerging Techonomy for decades.

Strategic Techonomic Resource: Electric Power

If natural gas and coal (and, to a smaller degree, the splitting of atoms) are the energy sources behind the Techonomy, electricity is the mother's milk. Think of it this way: electrons = bytes of data. We draw electricity into our computers, phones, and digital appliances and convert the electrons into bits of information that are stored in machines powered by ... more electricity. Then we use even more electricity to transport this data on the backs of electrically generated waves of light (photons) around the Internet. The emerging Techonomy runs on super-clean electric power (i.e., 24/7, zero surge) that is available 99.99999% of the minutes of every year (except in California, where an attempt to socialize the power industry has met its predictable demise, with disastrous power shortages).

If the amount of data created by people and businesses doubles every 100 days, then demand for electricity is locked into a fundamentally expanding growth curve as well. More data equals more electric power consumed. The digital infotech ecosystem is now estimated to consume 3% to 5% of *all* the electrical power generated in the United States, according to most experts—and some estimate it as high as 8%.

Exploding Techonomic growth results in exploding e-power demand.

Tech-Centric Real Estate

As we move up the Techonomy food chain from natural gas and electric power, we arrive at the other core building block of the Techonomy foundations: brainpower. And brainpower needs a place to hang out. Although virtual business is a reality, most Techonomy business is collaborative— we need to talk and think out loud with other people to succeed. Video conferences have their place, but the innate human need to think out loud and interact with other human beings is an irreplaceable aspect of the Techonomy built on ideas.

This means that office, R & D, and industrial real estate located within the regional Techonomy centers (e.g., Silicon Valley, Silicon Alley, the greater Washington, D.C., area) are strategic resources in this new Techonomy.

Education and Learning Services

All that brainpower within our Techonomy requires constant learning to stay competitive. Traditional educational institutions only *start* Techonomy professionals on a lifelong path of learning. Postgraduate infotech training and education are key enabling resources, as well.

Semiconductors

Just as cheap and abundant oil was the lifeblood of the last leg of the industrial revolution, semiconductors are the lifeblood of the Techonomy. Ever-faster, ever-cheaper, ever-more-powerful semiconductors (made possible by ever-more-powerful semiconductor-manufacturing equipment) make innovative information technology possible. The annual growth rate of the semiconductor industry has averaged 17% a year for more than twenty years. There is no viable argument for claiming that this growth rate will diminish in the foreseeable future.

DataTone and StorageTone Infrastructure and Services

Just like dial tone in the industrial age, the new Techonomy data serving and storage is too critical to business to be managed part time. Data storage resides both on and off premises within vast server "farms" and storage area networks. The data is transported via high-speed networking equipment and fiber-optic networks—the "plumbing" of the Techonomy—and high-speed-communication integrated circuits far different in design and use from their distant cousin, the PC chip.

EverNet Equipment and Services

Connecting all the data packet servers, routers, switches, PCs, wireless phones, and Internet appliances together into a single worldwide optical network is the job of EverNet connectivity services. Either wireline or wireless, every business and consumer will be connected to each other with all the knowledge of the world a click away. These wireline and wireless connectivity services are the toll roads of the Techonomy.

Data Security

Keeping prying eyes out of private and proprietary data bits is just as important as keeping the world's physical highways safe for passage. Encryption, server protection, user validation, and other "trust services" are to the Techonomy what the Brinks truck was to the old economy.

Distributed Manufacturing

The infotech and telecom products that make up the plumbing, computing, and communication devices of the Techonomy will be manufactured outside the walls of the companies who "make" them. The 24/7 contract manufacturing assembly lines and their real-time supply chains will become the dominant manufacturing engine.

Software Infrastructure

The Techonomy runs on software. Within our offices and contract production facilities, we take data from servers and manage/array it using server software and software applications that reside in electrically powered servers, data storage facilities, PCs, and wireless Internet appliances. We convert data into knowledge, algorithms, formulas, copyrighted and patented processes, and intellectual property that we use to create value for customers and profits for shareholders.

Digital Entertainment, Information Content, and Knowledge Content

All recorded entertainment and informational content will be digitally recorded, mastered, transmitted, and sold 24/7 in the new Techonomy.

Games, sex, sports, and other forms of entertainment will be transmitted via packets of data bits pushed through the air or over fiber-optic cable to our homes, offices, PCs, TVs, wireless phones, and who knows what types of other digital appliances. Critical information and knowledge will be appended to products and services conveyed through the air and over fiber optics.

Medicine and Medical Technology Infrastructure

The Techonomy also impacts medicine as traditional medicine is transformed by "molecular medicine." By the end of the decade, traditional medicine's drugs meant to treat disease symptoms will be genetically modified and improved via information technology and billions of dollars spent on breakthrough research to directly treat the *causes* of disease. All patient and medical data will be stored in digital form and readily available to authorized users in the blink of an eye.

THE NET RESULT: THE NEW TECHONOMY IS THE HIGHEST-PROFIT/LOWEST-INFLATION ECONOMY IN THE WORLD

According to J. P. Morgan statistics, the majority of profit generated within the seven largest industrial powers since 1990 has already shifted to the United States. Today the U.S. share of corporate profits is *twice* its share of world GDP.

And this world profit shift is accelerating—even with the 2001 recession. Let's do the math on just the infotech industry's basic learning curve economics.

The Economic Laws of The Techonomy

Moore's Law, which states that the number of transistors on a microprocessor will double every 18 months. (I would add that, as a result, the cost of computing power drops every year.)

Gilder's Law, which states that bandwidth (the amount of data you can move through a circuit in a second) grows *three* times as fast as Moore's Law.

Packet Switching, which states that the amount of data packets transmitted doubles every 12 months, while the cost drops 100% per year.

In addition, optical fiber capacity doubles every 6 months, while cost measured by bandwidth drops 200% per year.

Basic Worldwide Internet Demand

Users double every 12 months—100% per year
Data bits double every 7.5 months, or 300% per year
Internet core doubles every 4 months, or 1,000% per year

The net result? According to Dr. Joe Davis at Seagate Technology, if one assumes that infotech industries will (not including Techonomy natural resources, electrical power generation/distribution, biotechnology, etc.) represent only *25%* of GDP by the end of the decade (a very conservative estimate), inflation, assuming a 4% unemployment rate and 4% growth rate, will be *reduced* by 7.5% to 12.5% over our entire economy. In other words, *deflation.*

And this simple equation does not count productivity increases baked into this new Techonomy. (That's because, as I pointed out earlier, no economist or statistician in the Fed has a clue yet on how to measure productivity in most infotech industries.)

What this new Techonomy means is that standards of living will improve dramatically for millions. For example, infotech product and service employees earn, on average, 73% more than do private sector employees today. They also produce up to a hundred times more per employee in profits than do Old Economy industries that are averaging 2% to 5% employee earnings growth. Nor does this forecast take into account the fact that U.S.-based companies own virtually *all* the key patents behind 90% of the most key enabling technologies behind the Techonomy explosion.

Bottom line: What the emerging Techonomy means to you and me as investors is that the economic future of the United States and other emerging techonomies is incredibly bright. The productivity embedding itself within our economy will make fools of those stopped-clock bears who disregard the incredible power of compounding growth combined with the ascension of declining-cost industries.

Ralph Waldo Emerson told us years ago, "Not in his goals, but in his transitions man is great."

MOORE'S LAW APPLIED TO THE U.S. ECONOMY

In a low-inflation environment, capital goes to growth stocks because that's where it earns the best overall after-tax, after-inflation returns. With low inflation come lower interest rates, which make the present value of a company's future earnings power more valuable because investors discount those future earnings at lower discount rates.

But why does our Techonomy forecast make the risk of economy-wide inflation (forget about short-term swings in energy or food price inflation) and stifling interest rates so benign?

Simple: What's happening to make our economy grow at significantly higher rates without debilitating inflation is that Moore's Law will soon become applied to a majority of the economy. As technology investing expert Mike Murphy says in his book *High-Tech Investing*, "Think of this phenomenon as 'learning curve' economics. When you add new information/knowledge to intellectual-property-based products and services, the new information gets into the economy primarily by lowering production and material costs."

Moore's Law tells us that computing power doubles every 18 months; at 30%–50% lower cost every year, that cost saving will soon extend to a majority of our GDP. What this means is the following:

A majority of our GDP is going to soon come from declining-cost industries. When declining-cost industries represent a majority of our economy, our economy becomes *structurally* embedded with substantially higher rates of growth and productivity with significantly lower price inflation.

Thus, the emerging Techonomy is simply the most ideal environment imaginable for investors in Techonomy-related stocks. It means that we have a future that will be more profitable with less inflation than we can realistically imagine.

The emerging Techonomy will be more conducive to growth investing success than any other period in economic history.

NEW TECH BEATS OLD TECH

Listen, when the Fed puts the brakes on the economy with contracting monetary policy and higher interest rates, the economic cycle always turns for the worse and our economy comes to a grinding halt.

And since the business cycle radically affects corporate profits and thus the amount of capital available for investment, all industries dependent on corporate capital expenditures suffer most in a contracting economy. Infotech industries are especially hurt, as I mentioned earlier.

But I do believe industries that comprise the Techonomy food chain benefit more from the new Techonomy. The losers in this transition are old-tech companies in basic manufacturing, commodity production, and low-tech services. Old tech in the sense that:

- Their products change slowly—cars, refrigerators, even air travel.
- They have little pricing power or ability to pass on higher labor costs because of global competition.
- Their only opportunity to grow earnings significantly is through merger and acquisition consolidation, followed by substituting capital for labor by investing in new productivity-enhancing technology.

Almost the complete opposite is true of services and products of the Techonomy:

- New tech replaces old tech, and newer tech replaces new tech, as technology becomes obsolete every 12 to 36 months—generating more unit sales.

- New tech does not worry about cost pass-through, because these companies learned long ago how to generate higher and higher levels of profit via increased unit sales, while dropping the price of their products every year as a result of increased productivity.
- New tech volume grows because its products increase customers' productivity—which in turn adds to volume growth.

Herein lies a formula for significant compound wealth building and the core logic behind my optimism about our future. What the new Techonomy means is the ascension of cost-decreasing/high-value-added/productivity-building industries and the contraction of cost-increasing/lower-value-added industries as a percentage of our GDP.

It is the best scenario you could imagine for investing in stocks with monster investment returns in the future.

CHAPTER FOUR

From Monster Change
Come Monster Stocks

Change is the law of life. And those who look only to the past or present are certain to miss the future.

—President John F. Kennedy, June 1963

The point of our emerging Techonomy thesis is to set the investment context for the two decades ahead. The good news is that severe or "monsterish" levels of change are mandatory for creating an environment conducive to monster wealth creation . . . and we have monster rates of change coming in spades. "Monster" growth stocks—the kind that grow 500% to 1,000% over time—don't come from times of linear or slow predictable growth.

For example, in the rapidly changing '90s, 259 stocks rose 1,000% or more—a lifetime of growth for most investors earned by one stock in 10 years. But the Top 20 monster stocks grew on average more than *27,000%*!

The rewards of a few monster stocks can be life-altering. With increases of 91,000% by Dell, 68,000% by Cisco, 66,000% by AOL, and 21,000% by Qualcomm, you would have become a millionaire five to ten times over in less than a decade with an investment of as little as $5,000.

Monster Growth Stock Investing

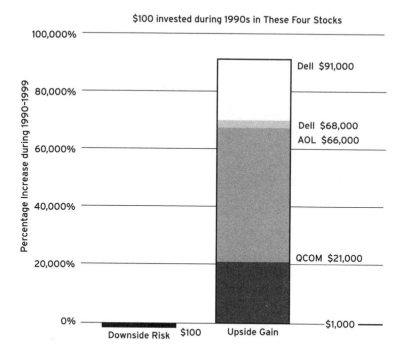

$100 invested during 1990s in These Four Stocks

Even if you disregarded the advice of my first book and held on to these stocks *after* they broke their 50- or 200-day moving average prices to fall 50% to 80% lower, you would have made a fortune, earning 10 times your investment.

We will undoubtedly return to more historically "normal" rates of stock market returns and valuations in the postbubble investment world. But the great news is that the increasing exponential rate of progress in the Techonomy means we should expect that even more disruptive innovations will hit the marketplace in the next 10 years than occurred in the past 10.

Don't forget that the monster stocks of the early twenty-first century will come from many non-infotech industries, too, like alternative energy, water management, natural gas exploration, and production technology, to name a few. ChangeWave Investing is about riding waves of change no matter where they come from—tech investing is only one sector of our universe of stocks.

THE RISK OF STAYING ON THE SIDELINES

Growth investing—and particularly *aggressive-growth* investing—is *not* a strategy for a majority of your investment portfolio. Those investors with 100% of their money invested in expensively valued tech stocks in 2000–2001 learned this brutal lesson the hard way.

But the most important reason to dedicate a *part* of your investment capital to monster growth stocks is the risk of *not* participating in this revolutionary age. With so many explosive markets and stocks, the mathematics is too compelling to dismiss.

When you aggressively invest a portion of your investment capital in the world's fastest-growing companies, the most money you can lose is 100%. Yet many companies profiting from the emerging Techonomy revolution generate investment returns of 1,500% to 3,000%, sometimes in as little as a few years. This means you could literally invest $1,000 in 10 companies, have nine stocks go to $0, and still make 10% on your money by catching only one 1,000% winner.

So think about this: The most you can lose is 100%, and there's a good possibility that you can catch a gigantic wave-riding stock and earn a return of 1,000%-plus. Is that a bet you'd want to take with at least some of your investment capital? Can you really afford not to be in this once-every-hundred-years game?

Building a million-dollar investment portfolio is a simple game. Thanks to the power of compounding (i.e., your money grows exponentially rather than linearly, because it earns a return on your original money *plus* its return as its growth rate accelerates each year), a 20-year-old need invest only $1,014 a year with a 11% annual return to have saved $1 million by the time he is 65.

A person at 40 needs to save $8,740 per year at the same rate. In other words, the 20-year-old has invested only $45,609 during the 45-year time stretch, while the 40-year-old invests $218,506. I can't imagine a better reason to start investing early.

Now here is where aggressive-growth investing comes in. For every

In the Twenty-first Century, Everyone Can Be a Millionaire by Age 65—How Much Per Year Will It Cost You?

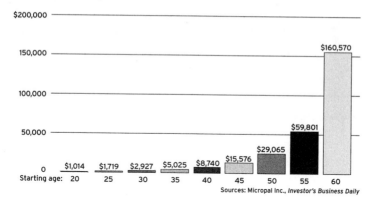

Sources: Micropal Inc., *Investor's Business Daily*

Total Invested by Age 65

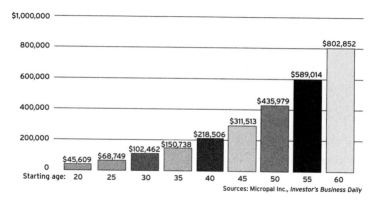

Sources: Micropal Inc., *Investor's Business Daily*

0.5% you add to your overall portfolio growth each year as a result of the 10% to 20% of your portfolio invested in high-growth stocks, you cut off about one year in attaining your $1,000,000 portfolio goal. Add 5% additional growth to your portfolio and you wind up working *10* years less.

CONSTANT COMPOUND GROWTH IS A DIFFICULT CONCEPT TO GRASP

The incredible wealth-building power of constant compound growth is too hard for most of us to grasp easily. Case in point: If I gave you a penny today and doubled the amount every day for 30 days, how much money would you have?

Try over $1 million. Compound growth sneaks up on you. In this example, it takes 25 days just to get to $100,000. But on the last day alone, you make $500,000.

Similarly, if you start investing with $5,000 and every day add just .5% growth to it, how much will you have in five years? Fifty thousand dollars? Believe it or not, it would be $3,000,000.

But here's the real point. The role of an aggressive-growth investing portfolio is to make a *minority* of your investment capital cut years and years off your working career by increasing the constant compound growth rate of your *entire* portfolio by just 3% to 5% per year. That's it. Every additional 1% your aggressive portfolio adds to your total wealth growth rate takes a half year off your "need to work for money."

Think of successful aggressive investing (what Charles Schwab calls "explore" investing) as your secret strategy for working fewer years and playing more.

Or do you *want* to work forever?

TWENTY-FOUR HOURS A YEAR IS ALL IT TAKES

Adding 3% additional return to a portfolio seems to be inconsequential. But think of it this way. Let's say you put up $10,000 in a mutual fund that earned 12% on your money for 30 years. You put another $10,000 to work and invest two hours a month searching for six to 10 ChangeWave growth stocks that average 15% growth.

You'd earn $320,000 more on your money for your 720 hours of work—not a bad return on your investment of time.

Is it too late to play the game? This question is a bit like asking a young Henry Ford in 1917, "Is it too late to invest in the automobile business?"

We have just entered the first years of a 20- to 30-year revolution that makes the New Economy revolution look like a jailbreak from a one-cell jail.

Given the fantastic economic environment of the emerging Techono-my, once we're past the bloodbath of the Nasdaq Techwreck 2001, you and I begin another cycle of multitrillion-dollar growth.

DON'T BET AGAINST 70 MILLION BABY BOOMERS' RETIREMENT MONEY, EITHER

Betting against the boomers' trillions of retirement dollars, and the 40 trillion to 126 trillion dollars they start to inherit over the next 30 to 40 years, is a loser's game. Why? Because a majority of that money is going into stocks—primarily because it has nowhere else to go. This is where the cash will come from to fuel the extended bull market we project.

Is the market risky? On a year-to-year basis, of course. But what pessimists continually fail to realize is that for the 70 million U.S. baby boomers (and an even larger number in euro land and Asia) furiously saving their hard-earned money for retirement, it's even riskier staying *out* of the equity markets.

And make no mistake—it's the boomer from the United States, Asia, and Europe (particularly when the euro becomes the currency for most European individual investors) investing in his or her future who is really driving the demand side of the stock market. To have a chance of reaching the amount of dough required to keep the BMW detailed and the frequent-flyer mileage up to snuff, boomers are doing what any sane person would do faced with the same situation. They are putting their money into the *only* thing that gives them a fighting chance for the future they envision and feel entitled to: growth stocks.

We all know the situation—boomer or not. Tom Monroy, a noted demographics researcher, calls the key group of boomers born between 1946 and 1955 the "EBREs—Early Boomers Redefining the Economy." Many of these "e-breeze" investors, freed from the emotional shackles of the Depression, accustomed to a taste for the good life, have no choice but to invest aggressively with their retirement money. Otherwise, given their age, they don't stand a chance of meeting their financial needs.

You need 60% of your preretirement salary to live comfortably in retirement, and many boomers know they are behind on their saving. And 4% to 5% interest from bonds ain't gonna get them where they wanna go.

DON'T LET THE OLD-TIMERS CONFUSE THE CONTEXT

Older pessimists talk about the fact that the 1960s and '70s bear markets portend a dismal future for the market. But they miss five enormous economic points about the twenty-first-century investment environment. (Forget about the emerging Techonomy argument.)

First, it was incredible that anyone invested in stocks at all during that time. Remember the marginal tax rate in the 1960s? Try 74% combined marginal federal and state at the highest income rates—including 50% capital gains taxes!

Why would anyone take the risk of stock investing—especially when you could get a 100% guaranteed return on your investment dollar buying tax shelters like avocado farms and oil wells?

The competition for investors' dollars grew even fiercer in the '70s and early '80s when tax shelters emerged with $10 tax write-offs for a $1 investment (thus saving up to $5 in taxes). Why *did* anyone invest in stocks?

Today, however, stocks are the *only* retirement game in town. It's also the only government-approved tax shelter left to the individual investor (hold a stock for one year and a day and get a 20% maximum tax rate on your profit). Bonds, which spin off 5% annual dividends taxed at 40% rates with 2% to 3% inflation, fail miserably. Real-estate-tax deductions can't be used against ordinary income, and no one has the time to be a landlord. Realistically, only the 8% to 10% historic return of stocks gets the boomer anywhere close to the promised land, and the boomer investor knows it.

Second, in the 1960s and '70s, much of corporate America guaranteed a healthy monthly lifelong pension (50% to 75% of your highest last five-year income average!) to anyone who did their 20 years of hard labor. Jeez—who needed to build a big nest egg *outside* of retirement plans?

Today, fewer than 5% of the boomers are covered by a traditional pension. (You lucky autoworkers you.) It's up to boomers themselves to fund their retirements. All of which places even more retirement money into stocks.

Third, the great shift of the world's profits has made the United States the dominant profit maker of the world. In the old days—1992, for instance—according to J. P. Morgan & Co., American companies accounted for 25% of the world's profits in the six major global economies. Today, that number is more than 40%—while our share of GDP is roughly the same.

Fourth, the U.S. share of corporate profits is nearly *double* its share of GDP—including the profit recession of 2001. Upon economic reexpansion in 2002, this percentage is expected to rise to 50% by 2005. Stock valuations *do* follow profit growth—and the profit growth in the world is in the country that owns nine out of ten of the key intellectual properties behind the world's growth.

Fifth, U.S. baby boomers are going to inherit *between $40 trillion and $126 trillion* of wealth over the next 40 years. Boston College researchers claim that "it can now safely be said that the forthcoming transfer of wealth will be many times larger than any generation by a factor of 10 over the previous generational wealth transfer."

Where is that money going to go? Where it is treated best and grows the safest—in well-diversified stock portfolios.

Ten percent market corrections come twice a year, and bear markets about every four years or so. But 70 million boomers' need for building a $1 million–plus retirement nest egg is not an option and remains constant.

Don't fall for the pessimistic claptrap of the bear market prophets whining incessantly on the boob tube about the "Big Crash-Dow 500" future ahead for stocks. You'll be poorer in mind and wallet if you do.

Listen, we've just had a once-every-other-decade bear market—and a tech stock bubble burst as well. However, it's worth pointing out that we started the '90s with $4 trillion in household wealth and ended with nearly $15 trillion—and that's after giving almost $5 trillion back!

CONCLUSION: THE BEARISH SCENARIO—
THAT DOG WON'T HUNT

To get a firm grip on the opportunity ahead, let me paraphrase investment strategist Ed Kershner of UBS PaineWebber. In light of all you know about the emerging new Techonomy and the world in general, do you really think:

- Structural inflation (increasing-cost industries and deficit-spending government) is coming back?
- Information technology and the Internet are going to be *less* a part of our economic future than they are today, or more?
- People are demanding *bigger* government?
- There is a reasonable chance of another world war?
- That Old Economy industrial growth will reverse and grow faster than techonomic GDP?
- Boomers will need *less* for their retirement nest egg?

In this context, it is easy to grasp the big picture of long-term prosperity and opportunity ahead. Don't let the bears scare you away from your coming fortune.

We have only three certainties in life: death, taxes, and increasing rates of change. ChangeWave Investing is all about learning how to profit and thrive from a radically changing world.

So now let's get you into the game.

A SPECIAL MESSAGE ABOUT
STOCK MARKET INVESTING RISK

Optimism aside, you have to understand a basic component of investing in stocks. You get the 50% to 100% higher returns from stocks over the world's safest investment (i.e., Treasury bonds) only *if* you can endure volatility. Enduring volatility (read 20% price swings) is the price equities investors pay to earn higher rates of return than bond investors.

Thus, the ability to endure volatility is the key element of successful equity investing.

A great hedge fund manager once told me that when it comes to day-to-day prices the stock market is 90% psychology and 10% fundamentals. Volatility or high/low price swings in day-to-day prices come from extreme swings in the levels of certainty or uncertainty about the future. (Specifically, levels of certainty/uncertainty about earnings power of companies, currency valuations, and levels of future inflation that would destroy earnings power, currencies, and present value of a dollar.)

If you are going to be a stock investor, and in particular hold aggressive-growth equities, each year you are 100% *guaranteed* to have at least one or two 10%-plus Nasdaq price corrections lasting on average 49 days (which means your aggressive-growth stocks will correct 1.5 to 2.5 times *more* than the average), and every four years you will have a 20%-plus bear market lasting between five and 13 months. Guaranteed.

You have to look at the schizophrenic nature of the stock market this way: Without these inevitable bouts of psychological despair, you'd never get a chance to make above-average profits.

You can't get it both ways—you don't get higher-than-market rates of return in stocks *without* getting opportunities to buy them at lower-than-realistic prices. Recent research by noted professor Jeremy Siegal from the Wharton School at the University of Pennsylvania indicates that of 120 of the biggest daily rises and falls in market history, only 30 had any direct reason behind the move.

Volatility is the tool we use to get *higher* returns. Period.

Said another way, the more certainty there is about the future of an investment, the lower the investment return. In investing, we trade certainty for the opportunity to earn higher returns from less-certain investments that eventually become very certain winners.

Now, we go through periods where people are *very* certain about the near future—and this makes them bid up stocks because they see earnings *much* higher in the future with stable economic (i.e., currency and inflation) risk. In highly certain economic times, stocks go up in value because optimism creates more people who want to own stocks than sell them. This is called a bull market.

The years 1995–1999 represented an almost "perfect world of certainty." Certainty that the Fed would bail out our economy with rate cuts. Certainty that energy prices were headed south. Certainty that inflation was doubly in check with a vigilant Fed and the new inflation-eating productivity being introduced into our economy with the $200 billion explosion of spending on productivity-enhancing infotech.

Only the impact of Y2K was uncertain, but it brought the certainty of monetary base expansion (the fuel of the Nasdaq bubble) by the Fed's dumping of more than $500 billion in additional cash (a.k.a. liquidity) into our economic system—cash that was not hoarded under the mattress but invested in exploding-growth Internet and tech stocks. The Y2K non-event also brought the money scared by the apocalyptic forecasts of a world gone haywire back to stocks in record amounts.

We go through periods where people are very uncertain about the near future—like much of 2000–2001. From the day Microsoft warned about earnings in March 2000, we entered a "perfect storm of uncertainty."

The Nasdaq crash of 2000 was, in effect, a crash of "good" economic certainty replaced with a mostly "bad certainty." For a terrifying and grueling 13-month period of history, we had no certainty of growth. No certainty of energy costs. No certainty of bullish monetary system management. Even no certainty of a president for 35 angst-ridden days.

And the bad certainty? The certainty of Fed interest rate hikes. The certainty of Middle Eastern distress. The certainty of Alan Greenspan pulling more than $500 billion in monetary reserves *out* of the economy to undo his overdone monetary expansion from both the Y2K scare and the $200 billion he pumped into the system to bail out the Long Term Capital Management fiasco.

All this uncertainty makes many people sell stocks and buy the certainty of bonds because they see earnings much lower in the future with unstable currency and inflation risks. When there is more inventory of stock for sale than bids to buy them, stocks go down in value. When everyone wants the certainty of bonds, they increase in value (as their yield goes down). Temporarily.

The only sure thing about periods of "bad certainty" flooding and "good certainty" drought is that they eventually reverse themselves in a free-market-based capitalistic economy.

When a majority of uncertainty dissipates, guess what? Stocks go up in value again at rates *many orders of magnitude greater* than rates of investment return from zero-risk bonds. Think of certainty and uncertainty as riders on a stock market teeter-totter. As uncertainty goes down, stock values shoot skyward.

As I'll talk about a little later, the greatest risk for investors is to disregard the role of the business cycle in this drama. But the second-biggest risk is not being invested in stocks when the market turns—because up to 50% of stock market gains come in gigantic bursts of upward price moves as the world slowly comes to the conclusion that the contraction phase of the business cycle is about to be replaced with a new reexpansion phase of economic growth.

Moral of the story: There is only *one way* to make long-term money in the stock market—riding the higher highs and higher lows of the price swings of the stocks of superior growth companies. All the while, you use the business cycle to help you change horses (i.e., stocks) to improve your positioning on newer, faster-growing waves of change that will lead the next upward market.

Why do the stocks with the highest *and* most certain rates of earnings growth go much higher than the average stock when times of uncertainty become clear? Simple: What kind of company do you want to own if you are certain about safe economic risk over the next 12 months—a company that grows 6% a year, or one you are convinced will grow at 30% to 50% average for the next three to five years?

If the value of a company is the net present value of its earnings power over the foreseeable *future*—not the recent past—you want to own the company growing its future earnings 10 times faster than the average stock!

The only way you screw this up is to do the following:

1. Sell your best growth stocks at the bottom and stay out of the market.
2. Take that money and put it into long-term CDs.
3. Miss the inevitable oversized recovery of the fastest and most predictable earnings growth stocks when the fog of investor uncertainty eventually lifts.
4. Go back into the stock market only after you can't stand the pain of watching the same stocks you sold six months ago now selling for 50% to 100% more than what you originally paid for them, and going higher.

The concept of volatility is simple if you look at it in terms of degree of forecastable economic certainty—let's say on a scale of 1 to 10, with 10 being extremely certain and 1 being extremely uncertain.

As investors move from periods of extreme forecastable certainty to extreme levels of forecastable uncertainty, prices of stocks move downward in direct correlation.

Here is the trick: If you believe in the ultimate power of global capitalism and the ultimate deflationary growth of our emerging Techonomy, then you have to believe in the growth and inflation resistance of the economy long term. If you do, this means you stay invested in equities for the long term (but actively and dynamically manage your portfolio according to short-term risk and reward elements of the market you will soon learn).

If you don't deeply believe in the power of the emerging Techonomy in your heart—*close the book,* sell your stocks, and buy 30-year Treasury bonds adjusted for inflation.

It is that simple.

PART TWO

Becoming an Expert Change Analyst

CHAPTER FIVE

Riding the Waves of
Creative Destruction

OK, so you know that you need to have stocks in your portfolio positioned to ride the greatest waves of transformational change emerging from within the Techonomy.

You know that a *part* of your stock money should be invested in both ballast-growth stocks (i.e., stocks with 25% rates of forecastable growth) and aggressive-growth stocks (i.e., 40% to 50%-plus forecastable rates of compound earnings growth) to raise the *overall* annual compound growth rate of your money enough to get you to the promised land years earlier than you dreamed.

Now it's time to make you an expert change analyst to make sure you know how to find and catch these wealth-building waves.

But first let's quickly clear up one misconception about aggressive-growth investing. Aggressive-growth investing is *not* buying the most expensively priced stock in hopes that it will become even more expensively priced in the future.

The strategy of aggressive-growth investing to me is about:

1. Understanding the dynamics of transformational change
2. Applying that knowledge to find the primary beneficiaries of transformational change in context with the entire universe of change throughout our economy
3. Trusting in the incredible value-creating power of transformational change by buying the stock of the best-of-class "change beneficiaries" at *appropriate* valuation to their future growth rates
4. Riding these waves of change until they begin to crest and it's time to "kick off" and sell
5. Being ever mindful of the business cycle and its effect on the short- to intermediate-term direction of the stock market and your growth stocks

THE RULE OF 72

Aggressive-growth investing strategy is predicated on the power of compound earnings growth. This is where the "Rule of 72" comes into play.

The Rule of 72 says that to find the number of years required to double your money at a given interest rate, you just divide the interest rate into 72. For example, if you want to know how long it will take to double your money at 8% interest, divide 8 into 72 and get nine years.

You can also run it backward: If you want to double your money in six years, just divide 6 into 72 to find that it will require an interest rate of about 12%.

Thanks to the beauty of compound earnings growth, a company growing earnings at 60% a year doubles its annual earnings every 1.2 years. Companies that grow their earnings 15% a year double their total earnings every 4.8 years.

All things being equal, which company do you think has a better chance of becoming significantly more valuable in the future?

Buying companies that can increase their annual earnings 300% to 1,000% faster than the "average" company is what ranking our "fast-growth" ChangeWaves is all about.

THE CHANGEWAVE INVESTING CENTRAL RULE

Here is the basic ChangeWave Investing thesis: Magnitude (M) of transformational change (TC) equals the potential for compound earnings growth (PCEG) and corporate value appreciation, or:

$$M \text{ of } TC = PCEG$$

Increasing amounts of profit deliver the high rates of compound earnings growth necessary for investors to perceive a bright future for a stock—and bid ever-higher prices for it.

In ChangeWave Investing, we are not in any way *indiscriminately* buying the most expensively priced stocks. We are buying the prime cut, the filet mignon, the crème de la crème leaders of strategically advantaged industrial spaces who, because they directly benefit from the highest magnitudes of transformational change, stand to generate the highest sustainable rates of compound earnings growth.

Should the high rates of compound earnings we project actually happen, equally high rates of equity appreciation—that is, rising stock prices—will follow.

Thus, the ability to judge the *sustainability* of high rates of compound earnings growth is *the* most important aspect of analysis to the aggressive-growth investor.

Which brings us to . . .

ChangeWave Central Thesis No. 1:
Monster stocks need superior compound earnings growth.

It is the superior compound earnings growth potential of the right kind of companies—the primary beneficiaries of high magnitudes of transformational change—that gets aggressive-growth investors to happily pay higher prices for your stock than you paid.

Our shorthand for this rule is: "The right stock in the best space (i.e., a strategically advantaged industry) wins." Why? Because growth stock prices follow earnings growth expectations. And when those expectations are met or exceeded, growth stock prices continue to increase. Always have, always will.

ChangeWave Central Thesis No. 2:
Transformational change is the most powerful variable
in the wealth-creation and -destruction formula.

ChangeWave Investing strategy is built from the premise that the most important element in fundamental growth stock picking (as opposed to chart and graph technical analysis) is an effective understanding of how transformational change creates and destroys the compound earnings growth rate potential of a business.

As I've said, discovering and analyzing the potentially transformational economic, technological, regulatory, or corporate strategy shifts we call ChangeQuakes (which can turn into the powerful waves of wealth creation and destruction we call ChangeWaves) is the most reliable radar system I've found for scouting out and finding monster growth stocks.

Why? Because transformational change is the most important ingredient in creating the opportunity for profit. Explosive profit growth comes from periods of higher rates of demand than capacity to fulfill. Think of an industrial ChangeWave as a metaphor for extreme cases of supply and demand imbalance—great levels of demand for services and products with limited amounts of supply. Periods of positive demand versus supply means the fortunate companies in the middle of such a demand explosion earn historically high rates of profit margins and net profits. These exploding rates of demand growth come from violent shifts or waves of consumer or customer behavior.

The corollary to this rule is that *massive* transformational change creates opportunity for *massive* supply/demand imbalances—and massive opportunities for profit. We continue to live in a world where the greater the magnitude of structural change within any economic organization (country, industry, or company), the greater the opportunity for the construction and destruction of profit, earnings growth, and ultimately corporate valuation.

In growth stocks, and particularly rapidly growing hypergrowth stocks (companies experiencing rates of 100% or more annual growth rates, or CAGR), the most important driver of stock prices is the market's belief that a company has created a unique, sustainable, and defendable way to capture higher and higher rates of compound earnings growth—*before those perceived earnings actually transpire.*

Since transformational change is what creates the opportunity for extremely high rates of earnings growth, accurate analysis of change becomes your most powerful tool in positioning your long-term investment money on the most profitable side of a radically changing world.

To turn you into a more successful investor and stock picker, we need to turn you into a first-rate change analyst. But don't worry—we've made it pretty painless and easy.

CHANGE ANALYST TRAINING 101: UNDERSTANDING THE WAVES OF CREATIVE DESTRUCTION

The first things a good change analyst needs to understand are the types of changes that occur in capitalism, as well as be able to discern which ones make you the most money. If you are interested in making great profits, focus your attention on transformational change.

We call the type of transformational change that creates market-moving investment opportunities "investable change." And the hallmark of investable change is the concept of low- to high-magnitude transformations, which we call "S-curve transformations."

When you understand S-curve change, you understand ChangeWave Investing.

Types of Change

Transformational change, or S-curve change, is different from all other forms of change. S-curve change starts out slowly, then accelerates or bursts, until it begins to level off. If you were to graph transformational change, you'd get a three-part curve like this:

The Real Shape of Change

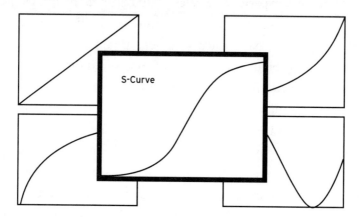

The S-curve describes relatively rapid change from one stable state to another—in other words, a transformation. When you plot the magnitude and rate of transformational change, it looks like an elongated S—hence the name.

Most People Misunderstand Investable Change

The picture most people have of change (as it relates to investment strategy) is wrong. Most people picture change as a line, almost always sloping upward. In other words, most picture *linear change,* that is, equal amounts of change in equal time periods. In the capitalist world, change never follows that path. In business, as in biology, nature always draws curves.

More important, linear change is what happens in slow-growth— that is, slow-changing—industries. These are business cycle plays and *not* growth investments. Buying Alcoa at the bottom of the business cycle

The Shapes of Change

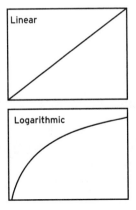
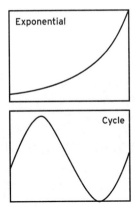

when no one wants aluminum may be a good short-term investment, but it's not ChangeWave Investing.

Other investors erroneously picture investable change as exponential change—that is, an upwardly sloping exponential curve that accelerates as it increases. This type of change applies to population growth and compound interest, but it is not the type of change we see in capitalistic activities, as much as stock promoters and dot-com companies want us to believe it.

Exponential change is unsustainable in a business—they simply blow up from too much growth. Although we experience periods of near exponential rates of growth in S-curve changing industries and businesses, the period of true accelerating rates of change is relatively short.

And, of course, we ignore incremental change. Here's why: Incremental change is like linear change—change that improves the status quo but does not transform it. Suppose you build a Ford Fairlane. Then you add tail fins. You still have a Ford Fairlane, only now it has fancy tail fins. Years go by, and you add air bags. Now it is a safer Ford Fairlane. But no matter how many modifications or improvements you make, it is, in essence, still a Ford Fairlane. Souped up, jazzed up, but a Ford Fairlane.

The opportunity for sustainable rates of superior compound earnings growth does not flow from incremental change.

S-Curve Transformations Are Tricky

According to Dr. Bishop, "The history of progress, though an apparently upwardly sloping smooth curve, is not that at all. Rather, history is a series of S-curves, sudden pulses of change interspersed between longer periods of relative stability."

Evolutionary biologists call this "punctuated equilibrium." Upon further review of Darwin's theories about evolution, scientists actually found from fossils that biological evolution showed extremely long periods of little change in species separated by relatively short periods of explosions in new species.

Transformational change happens in fits and starts as well.

If you look at human travel as a series of S-curve transformations, each lead technology was an S-curve of development as it was refined and diffused through society. Each technology has a limit, however, beyond which no amount of refinement would allow it to go. Every S-curve transformation has a point where the world becomes saturated with the new technology or the technology reaches its maximum capabilities and growth levels off to eventually flat-line.

This is where your understanding of S-curve change, the investable transformations we call ChangeWaves, works wonders.

How We Get Rich off the Big Mistakes in S-Curve-type Transformations

Most investors make two critical errors in forecasting the future of S-curve–type transformations. When you really understand S-curve transformational change, you won't. And your insight can make you rich.

Significance Precedes Momentum: The Lily Pond

In explosive S-curve transformations, a slow-growing but crucial base of critical mass must first be developed. This is the "foundational" period. The idea is best imagined by thinking about how a lily pond develops.

Kevin Kelly writes about S-curve dynamics in his book *New Rules for the New Economy*. Kelly's thesis is that biology is a better metaphor for understanding transformational change than is traditional Newtonian or linear economics. I, of course, could not agree more.

Kelly points out that in any successful business or industry there is a *tipping point* reached at which success feeds upon itself. The concept of tipping points comes from epidemiology; it is the point at which a disease has infected enough hosts that it has become a raging epidemic. This is where the contagion's momentum (which has pushed uphill against all odds) is now rolling downhill, with all the odds now behind it.

In the internetworked global market we now live in, the threshold of significant change is much lower than that of the old unconnected world. By the time a new technology has hit the tipping point, a significant amount of the money to be made investing in it has been made.

This is why, in ChangeWave Investing, we look for signs of significant transformations *before* they hit their tipping point, when all the world sees the change. The clues we look for are what we call "ChangeQuakes," which I'll explain more fully below.

That takes us to the lily pond parable. Says Kelly, "On a pond in summer a floating lily leaf doubles in size every day until it covers the entire surface of water. The day before it completely covers the pond, the water is only half covered, and the day before that, only a quarter covered, and the day before that, only a measly eighth. While the lily grows imperceptibly all summer long, only in the last week of the cycle would most bystanders notice its 'sudden' appearance. By then, it is far past its tipping point."

His point (pardon the pun) is that today's internetworked economy now works like a lily pond. To most, our economic pond looks empty, but there are many lily ponds of capitalism (new industries or restructured companies) quietly out there doubling in significance as rapidly as if they were a biological entity.

This is the bottom of the S-curve—the foundational period—which is the most significant and profitable time to invest in transformational change. The confusing part in discovering or validating the existence of a foundational S-curve being formed (i.e., investing in ChangeWaves) is . . .

All the Experts Will Be Wrong!

In the slower-growth, initial disbelief phase of S-curve transformations—that is, the slow foundational run-up to the fast-growth breakout stage—most people unfamiliar with the dynamics of S-curve change underestimate the degree or rate at which an industry, a company, or an economy can change.

History is full of examples. Oil forecasters in the 1970s could not imagine $30-per-barrel oil; PC manufacturers in 1983 could not imagine 1-GHz, 10-gigabyte computers costing less than the original PC.

The enormous gravity of what I call "anchored context" in the world's smartest people manifests itself in their complete failure to see past their existing reality. This anchored context phenomenon—being blinded by the truth you know today—is absolutely spectacular in its power. Consider these examples:

"Who the hell wants to hear actors talk" was a famous line from H. M. Warner in 1927. "I think there is a market for maybe five computers," said Tom Watson, chairman of IBM, in 1943. "There is no need for any individual to have a computer in their home," said Ken Olson, president of Digital Equipment Corp., in 1977. (Wonder why Digital went feet up?)

My favorite line is from Charles H. Duell, commissioner of the U.S. Patent Office, who in 1899 said, "Everything that can be invented *has* been invented."

You get the point.

Forecasting errors

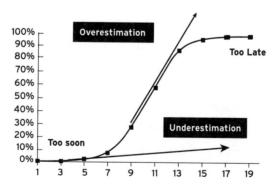

CRITICAL PROFIT-MAKING ERROR NO. 1: UNDERESTIMATION

In the early stages of S-curve growth, you as a ChangeWave investor must count on *all* the experts being wrong. Why? Human nature and the basic psychology of change. Experts are anchored in the logic and reasoning of their current frame of reference—that is, their past experience. Experts unaware of S-curve–like transformations have always misforecast—underforecast—the magnitude and effect of the transformational change.

ChangeWave investors count on this disbelief stage in our investment analysis. Indeed, it is the disbelief stage where the seeds of monster wealth are sown.

The most recent example of this underestimation phenomenon was the S-curve–like eruption of initial dial-up Internet usage. Early forecasts about usage, penetration, and adoption rates were all terribly wrong and grossly underestimated. An experienced change analyst would have expected this to happen and invested accordingly.

The huge wave of online adoption that resulted from the introduction of disruptive technologies, or ChangeQuakes, that spawned the killer Internet applications like e-mail and the Netscape browser was predictable using classic S-curve analysis.

Or think of a company like AES Power, which exploded its old structure and replaced it with a radically new one. For years, the company's open or distributed style of decision making in the electrical-power-generation business was ridiculed by those who knew the "old company."

"It will never work" was all I heard about the radical strategic shift in their business.

When AES became the largest independent electrical energy company in the world, I swear I still heard the "experts" say it would never work.

ChangeWave investors try to load up on stocks during the early foundational stages of S-curve growth when others fail to recognize the signals. I like to call this incredibly profitable moment in an investor's life the "blinding flash of the not-yet-obvious."

FUD Is a Good Thing

Of course, the fact that a majority of people—investors, portfolio managers, and institutions—don't understand S-curve transformations is a good thing. In fact, a large part of our success in ChangeWave Investing depends on human nature and the FUD (fear, uncertainty, and doubt) that accompanies all high-magnitude transitions.

Thankfully for us, the fact is that people recognize and respond to radical change differently, something that is as hardwired into our individual personalities as are our levels of smell and touch. This phenomenon is known as the Law of Disruption. First identified by consultants Larry Downes and Chunka Mui, the law postulates that where "social systems [read: "people"] improve incrementally, technology improves exponentially." In other words, there will always be a gap between those who grasp the "new" early on, and the pragmatists waiting for "clear evidence" before they accept that change has actually occurred.

The Law of Disruption means we can have an edge in our personal wealth building during times of great disruption or transformational change. Because, as aggravating as it can be to work with head-in-the-sand Luddites, there is a marvelous silver lining. Without the head start we get from pragmatic late-adopters to irreversibly transforming economies, industries, or companies, our investment results would not be nearly as dramatic.

The Breakout Stage: The Investment Sweet Spot

From the disbelief stage of S-curve transformations, we hit the breakout phase. This is the part of the S-curve where it goes from moving sideways to moving steeply upward.

This is the "knee" of the S-curve, and it's the safest time to invest in radical change.

In any S-curve transformation, whether it's natural gas prices or hog bellies or Internet adoption rates, the chart of radical rates of change looks the same.

The Investment Sweet Spot

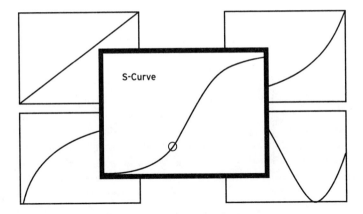

Strategic Inflection Points and S-Curves

In his classic book *Only the Paranoid Survive*, Andy Grove, chairman of Intel, uses the mathematical term "strategic inflection point" to describe the knee, or upward slope, of the S-curve. "A strategic inflection point is when the balance of forces shifts from the old structure, from the old ways of doing business, to the new . . . it is a point where the change curve has subtly but profoundly changed, never to change back to the old again."

In ChangeWave Investing, when the S-curve goes from flat growth and turns steeply upward, we have hit the strategic inflection point. Catch a wave too early and you go nowhere. Catch a wave too late and you miss it altogether.

It's easier for most nonmath people to understand the concept of the ChangeWave than the mathematics of S-curves and inflection points. But they are identical and represent the most lucrative time to invest. The early stage of change has been laid and the explosive growth is about to begin—and enter the radar screen of other investors.

The Morgan Stanley Internet Index Chart that follows illustrates what I mean. Anytime you see a chart like this, you are observing an S-curve transformation. But whatever you call these charts, the point is that they say the same thing: Big change is ahead. As an investor, you disregard this at your own peril.

The Internet Tidal Wave

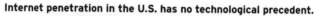

Internet penetration in the U.S. has no technological precedent.

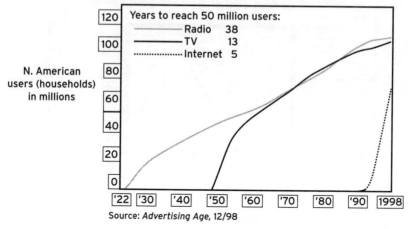

Source: *Advertising Age,* 12/98

CRITICAL PROFIT-MAKING ERROR NO. 2: OVERESTIMATION

From start to peak, S-curve change—or what we call ChangeWaves—can last for years. The steep upward leg, or growth period, of fundamental shifts in technology platforms like the PC ChangeWave lasted 15 years. In fact, major fundamental technological shifts historically go in 10- to 15-year cycles. This means the transition from client/server platform to Internet-based computing has a very long upward slope.

Industry-specific ChangeWaves typically last three to five years, and corporate ChangeWaves can last even longer.

But all ChangeWaves in their steep, upward-sloped hypergrowth stages eventually suffer the problem opposite to the underestimation phenomenon: the overestimation phase. When previously skeptical experts become entrenched believers in the previously unbelievable transformation, their once-anchored imaginations become "unanchored" and they replace old logic with new logic to understand what they are observing. This new logic phase causes the experts to overestimate the result, as you will soon see.

Once oil hit $30 a barrel, it was not hard to imagine $80 to $100-per-barrel prices—which many experts did. Once the Nasdaq hit 5,000, CNBC threw a party in downtown New York City and got a bunch of its market pundits on top of a bus calling for "Next stop—Nasdaq 10,000." A popular book in 1999 was *Dow 100,000: Fact or Fiction?*

The key point you must understand in analyzing ChangeWaves is this: What follows every, repeat *every*, hypergrowth phase of S-curve transformations is the "flattening phase." This is the point where saturation starts to set in and the growth engine runs out of fuel.

S-curve transformation, just like an ocean wave, hits a peak and flattens, without exception. By definition, when most everyone who could own a PC owned one, the PC S-curve/ChangeWave flattened. When everyone who was brash enough to buy an Internet stock had bought all they could buy, the market for Internet stocks was saturated and peaked, too. There are no endless waves.

The flattening of the S-curve is the equivalent of the surfer ending his ride on a wave. As all of us board or body surfers know, you ride the wave as it grows and you kick out *before* it reaches its crest and starts to crash. In surfing, hanging on too long is called "going over the falls." In investing, riding a winning ChangeWave too long is called snatching defeat from the jaws of victory.

ChangeWave Investing Helps You Understand When It Is Time to Quit Riding a ChangeWave and Look for New Ones

As an S-curve–trained change analyst, you would have seen the flattening curve of oil prices in the early '80s and concluded we had reached an anchored point of overestimation and gone short on oil. You would have made a fortune as oil returned to $20 two years later. You would have done the same trade as interest rates rocketed from 8% to 25% in six months in 1982—and retired with millions by buying municipal bonds as the interest rate S-curve indicated a saturated market for bond buyers.

When you looked at the S-curve growth rate of the Nasdaq or of infotech spending, you would have seen the almost-exponential upward slope of the S start to flatten in March and April of 2000—everyone who could have bought tech stocks *had* bought tech stocks.

Extreme visions of grandeur during every transformational change mean newly minted beliefs cause people (especially "experts") to over-project current growth rates to unreachable horizons. Sooner or later, every S-curve transformation, even the most wide-scale, falls under the weight of its own success. The market becomes saturated and demand levels off. In short, everyone who *could* buy *did* buy.

We saw this saturation point in the PC industry in early 2000. Heavily saturated markets for PCs and the slowing S-curve of PC growth told us to sell Dell, Microsoft, and Intel many months before the general public got wind of slowing demand. Ditto optical networking.

It's at the flattening part of the S-curve—when the experts are most prone to overestimating growth and demand—that ChangeWave investors "kick off" the industry and its leading stocks and look for a new wave. (It's also possible to make money shorting these cresting Change-Wave stocks, betting they go down in value.)

The Shakeout Stage: Time to Kick Off the Wave

The flattening phase of an industrial S-curve is the ugly part. This shake-out pattern has been repeated hundreds of times in economic history—the dot-com meltdown is just the latest in a long history of boom-to-bust industries and stocks.

Look at the auto industry. Do you remember the Pierce-Arrow, DeSoto, or Rambler? Here's why you don't:

In 1910, 15 years after the industry's birth, there were 275 U.S. car-makers. But by 1925 there were just 80 left. That's a 70% drop in just 15 years despite annual growth topping 24%. Today, in the United States, we have the Big Three. Same with ethical (prescription) drug companies. There were 152 firms two decades ago. Now there are fewer than 40, while growth has continued at 12% a year.

New industries are basically experiments. Professors Steve Keppler of Carnegie Mellon University and Kenneth Simons of Royal Holloway College researched industrial shakeouts and say they "are part of a competitive process in which the most able early entrants achieve dominant market positions through innovation." Their research shows that the survivors of new industries are the companies that get to greater than 10% share of their markets first—a fact we will use later in our investing strategy.

Disruptive Change: The Perfect Storm of S-Curves

Professor Clayton Christianson of Harvard popularized the concept of "disruptive change" to articulate a rare but powerful form of change that has very elongated S-curve tendencies. Disruptive change is rare because its technology results not in a new killer application but in a *worse* product performance initially. These technologies initially appeal to fringe customers at first and not the biggest buyers. The PC was a disruptive tech to the mainframe. Transistors were disruptive to the vacuum tube. HMOs were disruptive technologies to conventional health insurers.

Today, cheap network-attached storage devices are good bets to be disruptive to traditional large-scale expensive storage networks.

The point is that disruptive technologies are simpler and cheaper. They are usually commercialized in fringe or insignificant markets at first. They are usually embraced by the *least-profitable* customer segment. But they become incredibly profitable when the needs of the fringe market become the needs of the primary market.

Very few technology S-curves represent truly disruptive technology shifts. When you find true disruptive technology, it is *always* a home-run investment. It just may take longer for the upward part of the S-curve to appear.

How Change Analysts Find S-Curve Investment Opportunities

By now you know that our term for S-curve or highly investable transformation change (and the extreme supply/demand imbalances that result from such powerful transformations) is *ChangeWave*. ChangeWaves metaphorically represent the rate and scale of investable transformation occurring at economy-wide (macro), industry (micro), or individual corporate levels.

In ChangeWave Investing, we primarily use these industrial ChangeWaves to help us identify individual "spaces," or subsectors, within these waves of change that most benefit from these periods of rapidly growing demand and spending.

Think Trends and Spaces

If you really want to achieve great success in growth investing, you have to invest in "secular" transitions or trends. Secular trends are noncyclical transformations unrelated to the economy or an individual company. The advent of the PC and the Internet, and the desire for wireless phones, are good examples of secular trends.

ChangeWaves usually are supply/demand imbalances or demand explosions *within* a larger secular trend. Huge trillion-dollar secular waves of transition like the trend to Internet-based computing or natural gas power plants create even bigger rates of demand growth for the key enabling components that are consumed during these huge secular transitions.

Huge secular trends create fast-growing subsectors, or what I call "spaces." What we do in ChangeWave Investing is use ChangeWaves to lead us to these soon-to-be-hot growth spaces. Then we rank these various spaces by our "attractiveness" formula and buy the leading companies within the hottest spaces.

How do we find these hot spaces? We use incidents of macro- and microeconomic transformational change that we observe to lead us to them. For example, the macroeconomic Internet ChangeQuake created huge demand for the networked data storage industry. When we find an entire industry riding a monster wave of demand, we look inside the industry to its food chain of subsector suppliers or spaces. The goal is to find the one or two spaces within an industrial sector that benefit the most from the entire industry's wave of growth. We call this "mapping" the industry by its subsectors (we'll show you how in Chapter 10).

Sometimes high-magnitude, highly investable transformational change occurs with an individual space itself—many times because of regulatory change. In this case, we look to the individual companies competing within this very special space to find the primary beneficiary of this subsector ChangeWave.

Our goal in ChangeWave Investing is to have eight to ten of these sweet-spot spaces culled from many of the most powerful ChangeWaves identified at any one time. Our strategy is then simple: Buy the stocks of the leading companies in the hottest spaces we've found.

Thus our motto: "The right stock (i.e., the leader/coleader) in the best space (the strategic beneficiary of secular change) wins." To find monster stocks, you first have to find monster growth spaces. To find monster spaces, you have to find monster S-curve transformational change.

CHAPTER SIX

ChangeQuakes and ChangeWaves

Obviously, the key to successful ChangeWave Investing is to be able to find S-curve transformations early—and be able to distinguish genuine nonlinear transformational change from run-of-the-mill linear change.

It is also important to be able to judge the duration of the breakout phase of a ChangeWave and see the deceleration point—that is, the time when it's right to kick off and catch a new wave.

The way we distinguish which ChangeWaves are the most "ridable" (i.e., that have the most investable spaces and stocks) is to look to what created them in the first place. The tough thing for most people investing in change to reconcile is that the causal events that result in ChangeWaves *precede* visible momentum. Infant ChangeWaves are hard to see for the unaware or uninitiated.

Our strategy for finding the most profitable ChangeWaves is to look first for fundamental, powerful, and irreversible economic, industrial, or corporate shifts—what we call a ChangeQuake. These are the events that launch ChangeWaves.

ChangeWave Investing Thesis No. 3: All things being equal, the general rule in S-curve or ChangeWave Investing is: The greater the magnitude of the ChangeQuake, the steeper or more powerful the S-curve transformation/ChangeWave that results.

CHANGEQUAKES

Because I am originally from Southern California and grew up in earthquake country, the wave of power released from a shift in the earth's tectonic plates known as an earthquake is a very real, very visceral thing for me. That crack you hear when an earthquake hits, followed by an ever-growing rolling wave of shaking, stays in your mind for life.

That memory is what drove me to choose the term ChangeQuake to mark the occurrence of new, *potentially* transformational technological, regulatory, economic, or strategic *capabilities* that can set off equally powerful waves of transformational change. ChangeQuakes happen within economies and industries as well as within individual companies themselves.

ChangeQuakes and ChangeWaves are codependent. A ChangeQuake is the metaphor I use to represent an irreversible shift in the structure of an economy, industry, or company that precedes a ChangeWave. A ChangeWave is the metaphor I use to represent S-curves of new demand or spending resulting from these irreversible shifts.

Once a genuine high-magnitude ChangeQuake occurs in an industry, company, or economy, the affected company or industry is never the same because supply-and-demand dynamics (or profit potential of the business) change. As is true in my native Southern California after a high-magnitude earthquake, when a fault shifts, the earth and all that rests on it is permanently realigned, for better or worse.

In ChangeWave Investing we measure the magnitude of each Change-Quake we discover by the intensity of the transformational change represented by the ChangeQuake and by the size of the addressed market in annual sales.

On our "Richter scale," a technological ChangeQuake that provides a company a two-year competitive advantage over competitors in an industry with $20 billion in annual sales is 10 times more powerful than the same magnitude of transformational change in a $2 billion industry. When you find a "high Richter scale" ChangeQuake, you are certain to see a powerful ChangeWave launched as a result.

Think of tsunamis, the giant waves launched by an earthquake in the ocean floor. From the epicenter, or ground zero, of the quake they start as a quiet ripple that grows and grows in power until they hit shore, crest, and crash. The bigger the earthquake, the bigger the tidal wave.

The goal in ChangeWave Investing is to put our money on the primary beneficiaries of the biggest and fastest-growing S-curve waves of growth in our economy emanating from the most powerful ChangeQuakes.

KEY CONCEPT NO. 1: THE FIVE KINDS OF CHANGEQUAKES

There are five types of ChangeQuakes:

Economic ChangeQuakes. These are economy-wide in nature and affect the entire society. The introduction of the steam engine was an economic ChangeQuake that resulted in an economic ChangeWave or S-curve transformation we know today as the industrial revolution. In short, the economics of the economy transformed. Thereafter, navigation on rivers and the distribution of goods were never the same.

The introduction of the lightbulb was another economic Change-Quake. Suddenly, night could be turned into day. Employees could work a second and third shift. People could read after they got home from work. Sleeping and eating patterns changed. Nothing was ever the same.

Another economic ChangeQuake was the order-of-magnitude change in communications capability that evolved as a result of the Internet, providing a new way to move data at the speed of light.

The microprocessor, integrated circuits, and the breakthrough technology of dense wave division multiplexing (sending dozens of different colors of light down a single fiber cable) combined to fuel the initial leg of the economy-altering Techonomy ChangeWave we are riding today.

Economic ChangeQuakes are rare. But they are extremely powerful and produce multiple investable ChangeWaves. Needless to say, the emerging new Techonomy is an economy-wide ChangeWave resulting from the commercial Internet ChangeQuake.

Technological ChangeQuakes. These result from the discovery of non-linear technological breakthroughs. Technological ChangeQuakes are critical to the formation of many industrial ChangeWaves. They have the potential to effect order-of-magnitude improvements in the status quo. An example of a technological ChangeQuake is the adoption of a worldwide standard for high-speed data transfer over copper telecommunication lines in 1996. This decision made possible an order-of-magnitude difference in data transmission speed, from snail-like transmissions over copper wire using a 56K modem to the ultrafast 1-MB-per-second digital subscriber line (DSL).

The introduction of gigabit (one billion bits of data per second) chips by Marvell Technology and others created the gigabit Ethernet Change-Wave in 2000. Spending on this high-speed, low-cost local area networking technology boomed 500% from 1999 to 2000.

Regulatory ChangeQuakes. These ChangeQuakes alter the rules within an industry and bring a new capability or potential demand into the industry or subsector space. For instance, when the SEC changed the rules of the brokerage industry from fixed commissions to open-priced commissions, we had a discontinuous change or ChangeQuake. When Charles Schwab packaged the capability into a new service called "discount brokerage," it created an order-of-magnitude (i.e., 10 times better) commission structure that attracted millions of investors away from their conventional brokers.

Later, user-friendly Internet connections combined with the discount brokerage services to launch the online investing ChangeWave. (See "Aftershocks," later in this chapter.)

Strategic ChangeQuakes. Such quakes occur, usually within an organization, when a new business model or process creates a powerful new capability. A company can then package this new model or process into an order-of-magnitude-improved "killer value proposition" that brings a unique and hard-to-duplicate competitive advantage within an entire industry. Dell Computer's direct-selling business model is a perfect example. The key to a strategic ChangeQuake is determining if the new capability is difficult or nearly impossible for industry competitors to copy. If the new capability is not virtually copy-proof, it's not a discontinuously changing capability. It's just another feature that everyone will soon emulate.

Strategic ChangeQuakes are micro-ChangeQuakes—they occur at the company level. They create rapid ChangeWaves of significantly higher rates of earnings growth within individual companies.

They can occur as order-of-magnitude shifts in executive leadership or strategic direction for companies with unique or proprietary capabilities. In this case, the ChangeQuake usually results from the hiring of a new CEO, like Lou Gerstner at IBM, or Michael Eisner at Disney in 1984. If a new CEO massively and irreversibly changes the strategic plan of the company to significantly enhance the power of existing capabilities, you have a strategic ChangeQuake. In such instances the company does not have a new proprietary capability per se, it just uses its existing proprietary assets and capabilities to produce a new killer value proposition that significantly expands their compound earnings growth potential.

A strategic ChangeQuake can occur when a company shifts its business focus from one market space to a much bigger and more profitable market space. A good example of a major strategic ChangeQuake is Nokia (NOK) in 1992. The firm was formerly a conglomerate that produced lumber, boots, diapers, and steel cable (to name a few of its products). CEO Jorma

Ollila exploded a major ChangeQuake at the company by selling off everything *except* cell phones and cell-phone infrastructure. By refocusing the business 100% at a high-margin, rapid-growth trillion-dollar opportunity from low-margin, low-growth targets, they captured about *$180 billion* in new-wealth creation.

Another example of a strategic ChangeQuake is the company Manugistics (MANU). They were in a great space (supply chain management), with 50%-plus annual growth rates, high margins, and a big multibillion-dollar addressed-market opportunity—everything we look for in an industrial ChangeWave. But their management was ineffective. They missed hitting their sales and profit numbers repeatedly.

They were replaced with a complete new team that was compensated with low salaries and millions of dollars in stock options. The new team revamped the entire sales organization and, with the incentive of the options, made sure their numbers were made. This strategic Change-Quake served to explode company profits and the stock price rose from $5 to $125 in 12 months—during the Nasdaq crash, no less!

I could go on and on. But strategic ChangeQuakes are strategy-related and company-centric—not space-related. But when you find a Strategic ChangeQuake occurring in a company that is also in a hot space, these investments are many times more profitable.

FADQUAKES AND FADWAVES

There is one other kind of investable ChangeQuake and ChangeWave—I call them FadWaves. FadWaves are caused by a different kind of Change-Quake: the emergence of a mass-market consumer fad. Sometimes the emergence of a new consumer product is seen by a group of consumers as a way to be cool—a very powerful value proposition that offers an emotional payoff (for a while) that many people can't resist.

The Pokémon craze is a recent example of a highly lucrative but short-lived investable FadWave. One primary beneficiary of the Pokémon FadWave, FourKids Inc. (KIDE), rocketed 1,200% in 1999 as it rode this wave. Beanie Babies and the premium cigar fad are other such examples.

Of course, the key to playing this game is to identify the FadWave as it is forming, buy the pure-play companies behind the fad, and ride them until every magazine and news show is telling everyone about the fad. (I'll teach you a technical analysis strategy a little later.)

Then you sell your stock. If you want, you can go the other way— short the FadWave beneficiary's stock and make money on the way down. I did this in late 1999 with KIDE—shorting the stock at $56 and covering it (meaning buying it back in the open market to return to the broker) at $29 (what I call a CrashWave play).

The latest FadWave was in-line scooters. I rode Children's Place (PLCE), a company that sold scooters, up to $35 from $8 and shorted it when every shop on Canal Street in New York City was selling scooters for $35.

PLCE closed the year at $18.

FadWaves are short-lived rides, but they are very profitable to ride if you know when to get on and get off.

AFTERSHOCKS

An "Aftershock" is a second-generation, ChangeQuake-like improvement in an existing ChangeQuake. A simple example of the power of an Aftershock is Moore's Law regarding the computing power of microprocessors. (Loosely stated: The computing power of a semiconductor doubles every 18 months.) ChangeWaves related to this capability enhancement are easy to predict—because every five years there is an order-of-magnitude improvement in the cost and performance capability of computer chips.

Today, the emergence of XML, or extensible markup language, is a second-generation capability following the HTML ChangeQuake of just a few years ago. HTML is the hypertext markup language that is the standard format for creating Web pages. It "tells" Web browsers how to display elements such as text, headlines, and graphics. XML is a smarter cousin of HTML. It's a method of writing programming instructions (called tags) that describe the data itself. In XML, a number is not just a number—the format specifies whether the number represents a price, an invoice, a date, or whatever.

This makes it possible for computers to automatically interpret data and perform all kinds of operations without human intervention. Think about an automaker and a parts supplier. The automaker changes the specs on his order for windshields, and the specs are automatically changed at the parts maker. That change is then automatically made at his windshield foundry. . . . You get the picture.

Aftershocks have a much higher chance of launching profitable ChangeWaves than does the original ChangeQuake. Just as the market is getting a grip on the ramifications of the initial ChangeQuake, the Aftershock capability often moves the transformation already in progress into its steep upward hypergrowth stage.

CHAPTER SEVEN

Killer Value Propositions

The "Richter scale" I use to judge the power of a ChangeQuake and the potential of the resulting ChangeWave is to measure the potential degree of improvement or obsolescence presently offered to the marketplace from the new value proposition resulting from the ChangeQuake.

KEY CONCEPT NO. 2: KILLER VALUE PROPOSITIONS

Not all ChangeQuakes result in imminent, investable ChangeWaves. Massive shifts in customer demand or corporate fortunes are not caused by ChangeQuakes themselves; they are caused when entrepreneurial companies turn ChangeQuakes into "killer value propositions"—new, order-of-magnitude improvements in the status quo. Nonetheless, new killer value propositions occur only as a result of high-magnitude ChangeQuakes.

ChangeQuakes fight people's natural inertia. Very few human beings have an inner craving for new technology or lust for new ways of doing things. What most people crave is a clearly superior way to satisfy their insatiable DNA-encoded emotional hungers and desires.

Marketers worth their salt know that, in free-market capitalism, customers change behavior only when they see a new way of doing things that appears much more emotionally satisfying than their current product or service. People get emotionally engaged from tangible ways they believe they can:

- Relieve pain
- Gain pleasure, hope, or love
- Satiate a material lust or desire
- Reduce or eliminate fear (safety)

Give people tangible proof of offering one or more of these emotional benefits to their personal or professional lives and they become emotionally engaged and driven to try the new thing.

Great marketers understand this emotional calculus and position their killer value propositions with emotionally relevant promises. They see consumers in emotional terms. As master advertising wizard Roy H. Williams teaches us in his seminal book on marketing, *The Wizard of Ads*, "Intellect and Emotion are partners who do not speak the same language. The intellect finds logic to justify what the emotions have already decided."

Amen. Truer words have never been spoken. Remember how you rationalized buying your first cell phone? "It's for safety." Right.

ChangeQuakes make killer value propositions possible. They are the catalyst for the creation of irreversible secular shifts in customer behavior and demand.

But ChangeQuakes (unless they are regulatory) aren't the final, packaged solutions or demand creation event themselves—the promises that people can't emotionally (or legally) ignore or refuse. That is the killer value proposition. In the context of growth investing, what I have found over and over again is that when there is smoke (i.e., a ChangeQuake or potentially discontinuous new capability), there is often fire (a new killer value proposition being created out of the new capability).

HOW TO IDENTIFY A BONA FIDE
KILLER VALUE PROPOSITION

Obviously, your ability to judge a new industrial or consumer value proposition as "killer," or merely "incremental," depends on the context of its potential to get large numbers of people or businesses to change or transform their existing behavior. This is the key ingredient to getting in early on the powerful ChangeWaves that form around large-market killer value propositions.

Here's how I separate the dimples from the chad. The basic questions that determine if you've found a killer value proposition are "So what?" and "Who cares?"

Specifically, how does your product or service:

- Relieve pain/anxiety/stress (emotional or physical)?
- Deliver pleasure or hope (direct or indirect)?
- Satiate greed/build self-esteem (create wealth, status, or power)?
- Reduce/eliminate fear/regret (provide safety, predictability)?

If a new product or service delivers for customers one or more of these emotional benefits (or creates the perception it does) in an order-of-magnitude better way (i.e., 10 times) than existing alternatives, you have found a killer value proposition.

A shorthand way to get to the killer value proposition is to ask the following question (I ask this of the CEO of every company I invest in. It's a great question for getting to the bottom of just about any business idea, too):

"Tell me exactly what it is that you *uniquely* do for people that they desire and find so relevant and indispensable to their lives, and which is so much better than alternatives that these people are willing over the long haul to pay you 120% or more of the entire cost of providing the service or product for them?"

The shorthand version of this question is "How do you make people significantly better off in ways they already deeply desire and will willingly pay for?"

The key parts to this question are "for people" and "they desire." What separates a real marketer from a wanna-be is understanding that all successful new products or service developments come from satiating/solving people's *already*-existing problems or deeply held desires. Most new products or services I see fail this preexisting desire test. Or worse, they attempt to solve a problem that does not even exist.

Try this question at the office. It's a weak-idea killer if I ever saw one.

If the answer I get to this question does not appear to be near an order-of-magnitude improvement or payoff to a deeply held personal desire (compared to existing services or products), I find the service or product evolutionary and not revolutionary. I don't invest in incrementally improved products or services. And if you want monster growth, I strongly suggest you don't either.

If the first answers are plausible, the next question should be "How many people are there who share this desire?"

Remember, the promise does not have to literally be a 10-times improvement—this is hard to measure in most cases. But it has to be perceived as a unique and difficult-to-replicate way to get the emotional payoff lots of people seek.

The Emotional Payoff

The hardest question for technology people or for nonmarketers to answer is the emotional payoff question. Every successful product or service delivers an emotional payoff that makes the buyer feel better in ways they desire. Every product or service. I don't care if you make radio-frequency chips or sell firewood, there must be at least one deeply held emotional payoff people are primary seeking. If your product or service seems to be the best way the buyer can afford to satisfy their primary emotional desire, they will choose it. Even in commodity industries that sell primarily on price, there is an emotional payoff. (We just avoid these industries because they are low-value-added commodity industries with low margins—i.e., bad investments.)

For example, the emotional payoff that most business-to-business (B2B) products or service decisions provide is job security and anxiety/stress reduction. Most B2B technology buyers want predictability or interoperability from their services or products because predictability and proven interoperability make most people feel safer and more secure in their jobs. The emotional payoff is a reduction in their personal level of work or worry.

This is why the personal computer didn't take off until IBM launched its version in 1981. Before IBM entered the market, managers of information services were nervous about Apple or Commodore or even Texas Instruments PCs. After IBM unveiled its product, all that changed. As most managers knew, "Nobody ever got fired for buying IBM."

Killer Value Proposition Hunting

So how do you use this to become a change analyst (or marketing strategist, for that matter)? First, find the emotional payoff of a new service or product and measure it against the emotional priorities of the people who are the intended market for that product or service.

If the service or product delivers a significantly greater emotional payoff for relatively little additional cost than the alternatives, you have a killer value proposition. This also holds true if the service or product delivers the same magnitude of emotional payoff at a significantly lower cost (25% or more).

Remember, what makes people change their purchasing behavior is the cost and the relevancy of the new service's or product's emotional payoff value versus the cost and degree of emotional payoff provided by already existing alternatives.

Killer Value Proposition Handicapping

To understand a product's or service's value proposition, you first have to understand the primary emotional payoff people are seeking when they make a purchase. Are they buying better sleep at night, less worry, more love, less anxiety—what is the primary emotional hunger they are trying to feed?

A product's or service's emotional payoff has to match the highest priority sought by most customers from its use—otherwise few people will buy it.

Next you have to gauge:

* How many people there are who share this emotional hunger
* How much they are willing to pay to get the emotional payoff they desire

Marketing and Selling

Figuring out what emotional payoff people value most and matching that desire to the primary payoff of a service or product is the basis of marketing. Communicating the killer value proposition and getting people to accept your value offer is the basis of selling. It's important not to confuse the two.

CHAPTER EIGHT

Discovering ChangeQuakes and ChangeWaves

How do you find ChangeQuakes? Simply understanding the *concept* tremendously heightens your awareness of ChangeQuakes and the likelihood of discovering them in your work life and business reading.

For instance, let's go to back to the DSL broadband ChangeQuake story. A member of our ChangeWave Alliance (a grassroots group of frontline Techonomy professionals we've organized to help us all hunt down ChangeQuakes) attended a datacom conference in Zurich years ago. The assembly voted on establishing a new high-speed standard protocol developed by a publicly traded company (Aware Inc.) as the new core standard for high-speed data transmissions over copper wire. I received an e-mail from this member disclosing the new transformational capability. It sounded to him like a ChangeQuake had occurred. In a quick follow-up, we discovered that:

- Aware held the patented intellectual property.
- The IP was a required piece of the killer value proposition that the DSL companies were about to offer to customers. (Ten times faster online service than 56K modems.) So I decided to invest in Aware. I bought the stock at around $5 and it zoomed months later to $80. (I ultimately sold it around $60 for a 1,000%-plus gain.)

The best way to discover ChangeQuakes is in everyday reading and business experiences—but only if you keep your mind focused on finding ChangeQuakes.

New Economy and technology industry publications like *Red Herring, Business 2.0, Discovery,* and *Science* are great sources of ChangeQuake leads. Other good ones are *The Lancet* (for medical and biotech discoveries) and *MIT Technology Review* magazine. The Biospace Web site at www.Biospace.com is a great source for biotech research as well.

Next, Techonomy industry e-newsletters and magazines can be very rich sources. The University of Michigan Library has a particularly good list of free industry newsletters at www.mel.lib.mi.us/business.

The National Institute of Standards and Technology (www.nist.gov) site, too, is a rich source of potential ChangeQuakes. It regularly identifies the best new research breakthroughs via its Advanced Technology Program. When NIST sees a new development that could become a world standard—a definite ChangeQuake event—they support the discovery with millions of dollars. The www.NIST.gov site was the source for the idea to invest in emerging technologies like CDMA from Qualcomm and new semiconductor materials from Cree Inc., to name two.

I tend to use the Dow Jones Interactive Publications library and Lexis-Nexis to follow up on the ChangeQuake leads I discover. These services cost money, but they cover a much broader and deeper database of articles than do free Web search engines. For free data searches, Google (www.google.com) is still the best I've found.

Another place to discover new ChangeQuakes is www.Change-Wave.com, where I edit a free weekly e-letter called "Wave Wire." We at

ChangeWave Investment Research, LLC, get reports of new Change-Quakes and potentially forming ChangeWaves constantly, submitted by our ChangeWave Alliance members. The e-letter, free to registered users, is a rich source of ChangeQuakes and ChangeWave leads.

MAKING MONEY FROM CHANGEWAVES: WAVE MAPPING

When you find a genuine new killer value proposition, a massive regulatory or technological shift in a major industry, you have found a ChangeWave. To make money off your discovery, however, you have to find the primary beneficiaries of this new wave—the links in the food chain of ChangeWave-enabling suppliers that profit most from the growing demand about to hit the market. I call this finding the ChangeWave "sweet spot."

The way you find these sweet-spot spaces is to "map" them or break down individual ChangeWaves by their food chain—that is, putting together a schematic drawing or map of the primary components that go into the final end product or service.

We map ChangeWaves by asking the simple questions "What things and services do the companies have to buy to deliver ChangeWave killer value proposition to the end user? What technological and service pieces are required for the product or service to be built or delivered?"

For me, the easy way to start mapping is to form a mental picture of a company or person using the new service or product. If the killer value proposition is a thing like an Internet router or cell phone, you need to literally look inside the box or product to identify the key components.

Then I simply "connect the dots" between the most basic component of the enabling product or service and the final dot—the customer.

Let's use the third-generation broadband wireless ChangeWave as a sample. (By the way, a great place to get wave-mapping ideas is www.howstuffworks.com. Marshall Brain runs the site, and it is *very* helpful in mapping. I also go to www.Whatis.com to get definitions of words and industries and more clues.)

Instead of actually buying a Cisco router and tearing it apart to map the broadband wireless ChangeWave, go to established geek communities like www.newsforge.com and www.slashdot.com. These virtual communities are great places to ask genuine geek types about the key pieces used to create end-user technology. There is an online community of experts around virtually every industry you can think of.

I then go back to Lexis-Nexis, Dowjones.com, and www.google.com with searches (with quotation marks around the keyword or phrase to search the phrase or word only) on individual spaces or subsectors within a ChangeWave. From that search I build a list of public companies in the space at www.Yahoo.com and start combing their news and PR releases for strategic partnerships and vendor relationships.

Wave mapping is like putting a jigsaw puzzle together—except the payoff can be life-altering.

When you think you have most of the pieces to the ChangeWave, separate the food chain of companies into their functional categories. In the case of broadband wireless, there are seven functional categories:

1. **Enabling Intellectual Property (IP) Licensor.** Many times the core technology of a ChangeWave is licensed to component manufacturers in return for a royalty fee. In the wireless narrow-to-broadband ChangeWave, Qualcomm licenses its CDMA technology to most of the basic infrastructure manufacturers. If the ChangeWave you are mapping has an enabling intellectual IP licensor that collects a fee from a majority of the end-user companies, you have a *very* strong company that almost always should be bought. ARM Holdings (ARMHY) is another great example of a broad-based enabling IP licensor; it licenses its chip designs to more than 75% of the communications chip makers riding the broadband wireless ChangeWave.

2. **Enabling Understructure.** Using the broadband wireless example again, you don't normally see the components—or what I call the understructure. The understructure includes

the parts you'd see if you opened your Cisco router, Network Appliance storage device, or broadband wireless phone. This is where www.howstuffworks.com helps. In the wireless example, I looked at the vendor announcements for the handset makers Ericsson, Motorola, and Nokia to get an extensive list of component players. For example, Texas Instruments is a dominant maker of DSP chips, which go in every cell phone. So, too, is RF Micro Devices (RFMD) with their amplifiers.

3. **Enabling Infrastructure.** In the broadband wireless example, infrastructure is the core boxes and software that broadband wireless end-user service providers have to buy to build a broadband wireless network. Think Nortel or Nokia. For software infrastructure, a little research reveals that Portal Software and Amdocs are the broadband wireless billing software platform companies of choice. No billing, no broadband wireless.

4. **Infrastructure Service Provider.** In many ChangeWaves there are companies that wholesale the end-solution service to end-user resellers. In this case, AT&T Wireless will undoubtedly wholesale its broadband wireless network through resellers like Cellular One. There are companies, like Spectra Towers, that lease wireless tower space to broadband wireless companies so that they don't have to go out and buy towers themselves.

5. **Direct Service/Product Provider.** These are the companies that actually deliver or construct the killer value proposition service or product to the commercial or consumer end-user. In our broadband wireless case, these are the wireless service companies like Sprint PCS and AT&T Wireless.

6. **End-User Interface.** This is the physical product that people use to get the benefit or service they can't live without. Think Nokia handsets in our broadband wireless example.

7. **Pilot Fish Beneficiary.** Sometimes ChangeWaves spawn companies whose sole function (like pilot fish, which live off sharks exclusively) is providing a service or product that has

value only to one of the industries in the food chain. I call these companies pilot-fish beneficiaries, because they don't always show up on most investors' radar screens, but can be very good investments. Wireless Facilities Management (WFII) is an example of this category. They manage networks for wireless network operators where the operator does not have a physical presence. The company serves *only* wireless networks—this is what makes them the "pilot fish."

LOOK FOR THE PURE PLAY

When I look at a completed map of the functionary spaces that make up a major ChangeWave, I start by trying to figure out which spaces (and then which company within those key spaces) are in the sweet spot (in other words, which are the primary beneficiaries of the ChangeWave). I eliminate the companies that are not pure plays on the ChangeWave.

Remember our motto: "The right stock in the best space wins the money."

The first criterion of "the right stock" is this: one that is a pure play on the exciting ChangeWave space you have discovered. By pure play, I mean the company gets a majority of its revenue directly from the product or service space. The idea here is that if you have indeed successfully selected a sweet-spot space that Wall Street falls in love with and must "own," you want to own who Wall Street is going to want to own. We'll get into this in more detail in a minute, but Wall Street's first move will be to focus on the pure-play companies in the sweet-spot space and eliminate the companies that get only part of their earnings stream leveraged on the success of the space.

For example, in optical network testing space—a sweet spot within the optical networking ChangeWave of the '90s—Digital Lightwave (DIGL) is the leading pure play. Agilent Technologies (A) is a huge company with good market share in its space but realizes only a modest amount of its total income from selling optical testing equipment. Which company made a better investment from the beginning of the optical networking Change-Wave? DIGL by far.

In almost every ChangeWave I've analyzed, you make your money with the pure-play leader/coleader. Ignore the partial play.

WHICH SPACES ARE MOST PROFITABLE TO INVEST IN?

The big mistake I find most investors make when they discover an investable ChangeWave is to bet only on the direct-service or product-provider players.

I invest only in direct-service providers at the beginning of a Change-Wave, because my research shows it's usually more profitable to invest in the sweet-spot leader who provides a mission-critical service or technology that *all* the direct-service providers have to buy.

When a major ChangeWave is forming, I advise investors to (1) "box-car" (i.e., put money on the two or three direct-service-provider market-share leaders in the early stage of a ChangeWave) and, when one of these combatants becomes the dominant market-share leader, (2) sell the No. 2 and No. 3 market-share losers and keep the No. 1 market-share winner. (More on this "winner takes all" syndrome in the next chapter.)

For example, in the online brokerage services ChangeWave of 1996, we started with E-Trade, Schwab, and Ameritrade as our direct-service-provider boxcar. I also invested in the stock wholesaler that they *all* used to make their trades—Knight Trimark. I did five times as well on our Knight Trimark investment as I did on the direct-service-provider play.

Remember, the ChangeWave sweet spot is usually the key enabling component space that (1) everyone providing the ChangeWave's end product/service has to buy/use; (2) is intellectual property–based (usually), which means (3) the service/product sells at high—more than 50% to 60%—gross margins.

There are hundreds of examples of this phenomenon. Microsoft and Intel are great examples in the PC ChangeWave. Cisco was the now obvious sweet-spot play in the Internet ChangeWave.

If you look at the best-performing stocks over the last 50 years, I guarantee that more than 50% are the dominant market shareholders of a major ChangeWave-enabling sweet spot.

Perhaps a parable would help you understand this point.

IN TIMES OF REVOLUTION, INVEST IN THE ARMS MERCHANTS

"Grasshopper," the old man says, "you have come a long way to find out how to secure your fortune. How did you find me?"

Responds the boy, "How else, Master? Google.com! I searched under 'richest and most handsome picker.'"

Says the old man, "You are a wise grasshopper. Here, then, is the answer you seek: Fortunes are won and lost in moments of revolutionary transitions.

"But in revolutions, one man always gets rich. He is the arms merchant—the one who sells the bullets and guns of battle to the warriors. When there is a war on, Grasshopper, don't invest in the warriors doing the fighting—buy the companies selling the bullets. No matter who wins the war, both sides must buy bullets. You will get rich.

"But be careful to invest in the arms merchants supplying the battles for the highest stakes, for these are the battles for which the combatants will expend all their bullets and armies till death or victory. Remember, also, that no matter which companies win the battles, if you back the arms merchants serving the biggest, most ferocious battles, you get rich."

MULTIPLE SWEET-SPOT SPACES

Obviously, in times of revolution, the "arms merchants" are in the Change-Wave sweet spot. And, if the arms merchant is supplying bullets and bombs to *multiple* revolutions or ChangeWaves raging at the same time, the merchant does even better. And if the arms the merchant supplies cost $30 to build and can be sold for $100, he becomes a very rich man.

The moral? All things being equal, investing in a space that acts as a key arms merchant to multiple industrial battles raging at the same time is the best investment you can make.

How do you find these special stocks? Sometimes when you go through the process of mapping the food chain of a ChangeWave you notice there is a key enabling space that shows up in multiple Change-Waves. The security software space is a recent example of a multiple sweet-spot opportunity. When I mapped the multiple ChangeWaves emanating from the commercial Internet ChangeQuake that erupted in 1995, I noticed an unusual thing. Almost *all* the companies that were delivering Internet-based services to end users were paying big checks for:

- User-security service from a company called Verisign
- Fileserver storage appliances from a company called Network Appliance
- Server firewall protection from a company called Check Point Software
- Databases from Oracle
- Applications from an application server powered by BEA Systems' WebLogic software

No matter what the top individual ChangeWaves looked like or the market they addressed, they all seemed to be writing checks to these companies. I even began to refer to these companies as "common-thread enablers."

Guess which stocks made the most money for me between 1998 and 2000?

When you find a key ingredient to multiple major ChangeWaves in progress, concentrate your time and money in that space. This is where investment fortunes are made.

CHAPTER NINE

Which ChangeWaves Should You Ride . . . and When Should You Ride Them?

ChangeWave Investing is really a simple game. Your ChangeWave training helps you scour your everyday world looking for evidence of new industrial or corporate ChangeQuakes. When you find one, you look for a killer value proposition that should spawn the kind of sustainable and highly profitable supply/demand imbalance (or, in the case of a corporate ChangeQuake, the likelihood of new rapid earnings growth) we call a ChangeWave.

You've learned to look inside these industrial ChangeWaves to uncover the key sweet-spot spaces. Within these sweet spots, you identify and buy the stock of a dominant leader or coleaders and wait for the world to come to the same discovery as you. If your judgment is correct, other investors will bid up the price of your dominant sweet-spot stock—much to your intellectual gratification and financial benefit.

But let's face one problem now: We all have a limited amount of time and/or money. With literally hundreds of ChangeQuakes and potentially investable ChangeWaves erupting throughout our rapidly changing economy, how do you cut your list to a workable few spaces and stocks?

Additionally, no matter how big and powerful a ChangeWave is, the bear market of 2000–2001 taught many investors that riding the right wave at the wrong time (e.g., emerging technology ChangeWaves) can be very hazardous to your wealth.

In short, owning the right stock in the right (but not-yet-profitable) market space is no match for a bear market.

So which ChangeWaves should you decide to ride, and *when* is it safe to ride them?

ChangeWave Investing 2.0 solves this dilemma for you with two strategies:

- Growth Appropriate to the Business Cycle strategy
- The ChangeWave Sweet-Spot Scorecard

These two core principles of ChangeWave Investing help you put your investment capital on the winning side of change no matter how good or how bad the economy or stock market.

THE GROWTH APPROPRIATE TO THE BUSINESS CYCLE STRATEGY

Our Growth Appropriate to the Business Cycle strategy is designed to recognize a basic fact about investing in growth stocks: Aggressive- and speculative-growth stocks riding the highest-growth ChangeWaves need a strong, growing economy to be profitable investments. This means investors in emerging growth companies that ignore the inevitable cycle of expanding growth and economic contraction do so at their own peril.

Think of this strategy as the equivalent of the green flag, yellow flag, and red flag warning system at your favorite beach.

Let's face it, just as there are times at the beach when it is unsafe to be in the ocean, there are periods of time—sometimes very long periods of time—when it's very unprofitable to own aggressive-growth stocks. Denying this reality by saying "I'm a long-term investor—I take the good with the bad" is a recipe for significantly underachieving your potential reward as an investor.

To paraphrase the late singer Jim Croce, you don't tug on Superman's cape, you don't spit into the wind, and you don't mess around with speculative-growth stocks when the storm clouds of economic recession are moving in. Here's why:

The mathematics of investing is very perverse. When you own a stock that goes down 40% in value, you now own a stock that must go up in value 67% for you to get back to even. A 60% decline means you need a 150% rise to get back even.

Returns Required to Break Even from Capital Losses

% Loss of Trading Capital	% Gain Required to Be Even
5%	5.3%
10%	11.1%
15%	17.6%
20%	25.0%
25%	33.3%
30%	42.9%
35%	53.8%
40%	66.7%
45%	81.8%
50%	100.0%
55%	122.0%
60%	150.0%

For reasons we'll get into shortly, the valuations or prices of stocks benefiting from rapid-growth ChangeWaves are 200% to 300% more volatile than the market overall. This means that if you misjudge the economic environment and the overall market loses 20% of its value in a recessionary bear market, your aggressive- and speculative-growth stocks will most likely drop 40% to 75% in value.

The good news is that, with just a little simple work on your part, you can largely avoid the major bear markets (and their brain-numbing declines) that accompany periods of economic contraction. In fact, when you get the hang of anticipating the beginning and end of these recessionary periods, you'll find that your investment results will significantly improve. The fact is that *every* sustainable stock market rally in the last 100 years began before the *end* of a recession.

IS THIS "MARKET TIMING"?

I am not talking about market timing or trying to guess day-to-day market direction. What I am advocating is dynamically allocating your investment capital between what we call ballast-growth and rapid-growth ChangeWaves in anticipation of the recurrent ups and downs of economic growth otherwise known in modern capitalism as the business cycle.

I strongly believe there is an appropriate time to own aggressive-growth stocks—and a time when it is inappropriate to own them. The reason most investment managers disagree with me on this subject is that the investment world is largely divided into two basic strategic "religions," or investment styles—as I'll outline below—that most professional investors are loath to stray from.

ChangeWave investors, on the other hand, following our Growth Appropriate to the Business Cycle approach, can profit greatly by exploiting the battle between growth- and value-style investing.

INVESTMENT-STYLE AGNOSTICISM

The investment world is dominated by two basic investment-strategy "religions": growth and value. Various studies show that both the value style and the growth style of investing (over 10-year-plus periods of time) have delivered about the same investment performance.

Growth investors pray exclusively to the god of growth, growth, and more growth. They pay premium-to-market valuations for proven growth companies with the idea that expected future rates of profitability and annual earnings make the price of stock cheap today.

Value investors pray to the god of finding companies at a discount to their assets as measured by balance sheet and income statement. Value investors try to buy what they believe to be otherwise solid companies temporarily selling at a discount to their true "value" because their industry or company has fallen out of favor.

Strict adherence to either investment strategy religion basically means that in bull markets growth investors do better, and in bear markets value investors do better. But the key issue is that both styles come in and go out of style in three- to five-year cycles. Three to five years of underperforming the market is too expensive a religion for me.

I preach a different investment gospel in ChangeWave Investing: investment agnosticism. We don't exclusively "pray" to either investment religion—we pray to the god of transformational change. Why? Because to do otherwise means you are guaranteed to significantly underperform the market when either growth or value goes out of style, which I find unacceptable.

This is where a keen understanding of the business cycle pays enormous dividends to you. If you want to be a successful growth investor in *all* markets—bull and bear—just focusing on high-growth ChangeWaves and stocks without regard to the boom-and-bust element of the business cycle is a recipe for the kind of disaster many investors experienced in the Great Techwreck Bear Market of 2000–2001.

On the other hand, exclusive focus on the value style in a rapidly expanding economy can doom you to underperform the market for years, as the 1995–2000 leg of the bull market taught orthodox value investors. (They underperformed the S&P 500 Index for nearly 50 months.)

I believe my Growth Appropriate to the Business Cycle, or GAB, approach combines the best of both investment-style religions. What I've found in my investing career is simply this: When the business cycle is

The Roller-Coaster Ride of the Business Cycle

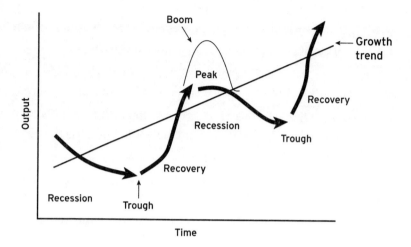

beginning to expand, the smaller companies riding the fastest-growing emerging ChangeWaves—the waves of growing demand that directly feed off an expanding economy—do the best.

Conversely, when the business cycle peaks and the economy begins to contract, our ballast-growth ChangeWaves and industries, or those industries whose growth is fueled by non-economy-related engines, do best.

Growth appropriate to the business cycle investing means that we (1) ride the "rapid-growth" ChangeWaves that do best at the beginning to middle of the business cycle (read: higher-P/E-valued stocks) when the economy is in fact expanding, and we (2) kick off those economy-linked rapid-growth waves when we get the key signs that the economy has peaked and move our money to ballast-growth ChangeWaves—the industries whose growth is fueled from largely non-economy-related ChangeWaves or industries that grow rapidly during times of rapid interest-rate declines.

This strategy literally saved ChangeWave investors millions of dollars as we started kicking off the rapid-growth ChangeWaves of the late '90s and their high-P/E-valued stocks as the dawn of the commercial Internet drove economic growth to historically high levels.

We sold many of our aggressive- and speculative-growth stocks at huge profits and put that money into ballast-growth stocks that continued to grow their earnings during the period of economic contraction that really started in October 2000.

I have consistently found that in investing it pays to be an agnostic, not an atheist. We *do* believe in the indomitable power of transformational change. We just don't believe there is only *one* way to make money from our beliefs.

(Side note: All this reminds me of the best definition I've heard of an agnostic. When asked about his religious beliefs before heading off to D day, a sergeant from the U.S. 8th Infantry was quoted as saying, "I don't believe in religion, thank God.")

BALLAST-GROWTH WAVES VS. RAPID-GROWTH WAVES

Investing appropriate to the GDP boom-and-bust cycle of the modern economy is why we divide the Techonomy industries and their Change-Waves into ballast-growth and rapid-growth categories.

As I mentioned, the goal of finding and riding ballast-growth ChangeWaves is to identify the sectors of the economy whose growth rates and earnings power are not dependent on strong overall economic growth. I call these industries ballast-growth industries in that the fuel of their growth is spending that's largely nondiscretionary by commercial and/or individual consumers. Ballast-growth industries are said to have a "non-economic growth component," and thus their stocks sell at a premium to the overall market in times of economic contraction.

On the other hand, rapid-growth industries, especially within the Techonomy food chain, are usually dependent on discretionary investment capital spending to fuel their high rates of growth. They are said to have an economic growth component and sell for premium valuations to the market in times of strong economic expansion.

Examples of ballast-growth industries within the Techonomy are natural resource industries like natural gas and coal; electrical power production and distribution; education; energy transportation; pharmaceuticals; biotechnology research and development; and health care services. In addition, times of economic contraction eventually bring significantly lower interest rates, which can create waves of new demand in industries like home building and mortgage lending. Growth in these industries is interest-rate driven. When interest rates drop significantly (2% or more), demand expands. Call these interest-rate ChangeWaves.

BUT INFORMATION TECHNOLOGY INDUSTRIES AREN'T CYCLICAL, RIGHT?

Wrong. The rapid-growth waves of the Techonomy—like the semiconductor, infotech, telecommunications, and most other high-tech industries—have become very sensitive to the business cycle and thus are economically cyclical (i.e., their rates of potential growth rise and fall with overall economic growth).

Why? As I previously mentioned, spending on information technology has become a large percentage of overall corporate capital expenditures (i.e., 50%-plus of capital expenditure spending). In fact, most infotech industries are dependent on the business cycle to fuel their growth rather than the traditional new-product spending cycles of the past, when infotech was such a small percentage of capital spending.

In short, in order for rapid-growth ChangeWaves to maintain rapid growth (and have their stocks live up to their high-earnings-growth expectations), they need the rapidly growing pools of discretionary capex budgets that come during times of economic growth. Follow the logic: A rapidly growing economy means companies with rapidly growing profits. Profit growth creates capital for reinvestment in productivity-increasing infotech—the software and gear companies need to meet expanding demand without increasing their overhead.

Most tech investors in 2000 forgot about the economic growth component entrenched within growth investing. They also failed to understand the concept of market risk.

MARKET RISK AND BUSINESS RISK

Another big mistake most investors made in the 2000–2001 bear market was to assume that other investors would continue to be willing to pay high prices (or what's known as "high multiples") for the future earnings of their favorite rapid-growth companies.

These investors learned a terrible lesson in the concept called "market risk." It was a very expensive lesson for many. Understanding Growth Appropriate to the Business Cycle will save you from making the same mistake, because what investing in GAB really does is give you a fabulous tool for managing market risk.

Let me explain the difference between business risk and market risk. Business risk is, of course, the risk of a company or industry failing or going out of business. Businesses in emerging industries also suffer from industry risk—that is, the risk of the industry not growing into an established industry, or failing to live up to industry hype.

CHANGEWAVE BUSINESS RISK CATEGORIES

The way we manage business risk in ChangeWave Investing is to rate each industrial or strategic ChangeWave in our universe by its business risk—that is, the maturity of the industry.

There is no mystery here: The longer the history of profitable operations, the less risky the industry or company. As you'll see later, we manage business risk in our portfolios by balancing the business risk of the companies you own to your overall risk tolerance.

We have four industry risk ratings (from lowest risk/lowest investment return potential to highest risk/highest potential investment reward) within our ballast-growth and rapid-growth ChangeWaves:

Ballast-Growth Industries

These are 10-year-plus mature nondiscretionary spending industries. (That means revenue growth rate is nondependent on strong overall economic growth—i.e., industries like natural gas and coal, independent power production, and generic pharmaceuticals.) We look for more than 10% compound annual growth rate (CAGR) with more than $10 billion annual marketplaces.

Rapid-Growth Industries

- **Classic Growth.** A 10-year-plus profitable industry with a projected 20% CAGR
- **Aggressive-Growth Industry.** Three to five years of profitable operating history and a projected 40% to 50%-plus CAGR with over $1 billion in annual revenue
- **Speculative Emerging Growth Industry.** One to two years or less of unprofitable operating history and 100%-plus CAGR with less than $1 billion in annual revenue

In ChangeWave Investing, like all other forms of investing, the highest reward comes from the highest-risk business categories.

We'll use this industry risk categorization all through ChangeWave Investing to match the return and risk you are looking for with ChangeWaves and companies appropriate to your goals.

MARKET RISK

Investors in emerging growth industries worry so much about business risk that they seem to lose sight of a bigger risk facing their money: market risk. I define market risk as the range of price-to-earnings or price-to-sales multiples investors are willing to pay for the forecastable future earnings/revenues of a company.

What I'm talking about, of course, is what Wall Street calls "multiple compression"—the risk of valuation volatility inherent in stocks valued at very high price-to-earnings (P/E) or price-to-sales multiples.

I believe that where investors made their big mistake in the 2000–2001 bear market was in not effectively managing market risk in their portfolios. Market risk can be extreme. It is separate from business risk. And it can be managed effectively through ChangeWave Investing.

Market Risk in Real Life

At the end of the day, all businesses are valued primarily on what investors believe their future earnings or revenue streams will become— not what they have been. You must understand that when a company is valued at a high price-to-sales ratio or what's known as a premium "market multiple" (i.e., one that greatly exceeds the average price-to-earnings or price-to-sales ratio of the average stock), this pricing implies rates of higher-than-average future revenue and earnings growth.

A premium price-to-sales or price-to-earnings multiple to today's average S&P 500 market P/E multiple of 25 (i.e., a current valuation, say, of more than 35 to 50 times next year's projected earnings) implies there's a lot of room for "pricing" in the stock. This is my definition of "market risk"—the risk that investors will no longer be willing to pay the same premium or higher-than-market-average multiple for a company's future earnings as you have.

What makes investors suddenly no longer willing to pay high earnings or sales multiples for a business? Two things: One is failure of a company to deliver the lofty expected earnings or sales growth. Failure to execute a business plan is part of market risk, and the issue is simple: Miss your numbers in a growing economy with a premium market multiple and you suffer an immediate and drastic reevaluation of the company's long-term prospects. (You'll also lose the premium market multiple in the process.) At the high altitude of premium P/E valuations, disappointment is met with an immediate 30% to 50% valuation haircut.

The second way investors lose their willingness to pay premium market multiples is when they conclude that the economy is headed for vastly lower rates of economic growth—in other words, when investors go on recession watch and expect significant economic contraction. When the economic tide is going out, the first thing investors do is jump off their high-P/E stocks.

THE GROWTH APPROPRIATE TO THE BUSINESS CYCLE MATH

Here's how recessionary math works against high-growth/high-multiple stocks sailing into an economic downturn. In other words, here's why it is usually inappropriate to own rapid-growth, high-P/E stocks going into the significant GDP contraction phase of the business cycle.

As you know, the fastest-growing sectors of our economy are the most immature relative to the economy in general (or they wouldn't be growing so fast—duh!). Why are they more subject to market risk than mature ballast-growth industries?

The answer requires us to spend another moment on classic stock market theory. Deep breath—here we go. The value of an immature or emerging-growth company is primarily dependent on estimates of economic conditions and cash flows several years out (as opposed to the cash flows of mature but relatively predictable ballast-growth industries today).

To arrive at a value for an emerging growth stock today, these cash flows are first estimated ("modeled") out five to ten or even twenty years. The estimated cash flow is discounted back to the present year (at an annual rate usually equal to the prevailing yield from zero-risk debt investments like short-term T-bills). Once a cash flow and earnings projection is complete, an earnings multiple is placed on the forecasted future earnings to come up with a stock price today.

Here is where it gets tricky. If investors strongly believe in significantly growing rates of cash flows in the future, they will pay a higher-than-market-average multiple today for the forecasted earnings of tomorrow.

(In other words, they will pay a premium P/E on whatever today's earnings are versus the average market multiple.)

Here's the key part: If the prospects for a company's cash flow or earnings are zero today and not projected to grow till many years out, just a little delay or change in future earnings expectations has a *much greater effect* on its present value than if it is closer in time.

In other words, relatively small changes in investor evaluation of the future (i.e., future cash flows as represented by current price-to-earnings ratios) have a *highly* magnified effect on the present value of the least-mature sectors and companies in our economy. That means premium P/E or price-to-sales valuations get cut in half (or more) the minute the future strength of the economy comes into question.

This is why getting the business cycle right is so important to investing in emerging companies. Immature companies (particularly tech companies) grow fastest (and thus get to positive cash flow earliest) riding the wave of an *expanding* economy. The appropriate time to buy most immature companies is early or in the middle of the expansion phase of the business cycle—when economic growth is strongest. (Immature biotech companies are an exception to this rule—their future cash flows are dependent on the success of their research.)

When the economy's growth has peaked for the cycle and started its contraction phase, immature companies' cash flow prospects get pushed farther away. Thus, their current or present value becomes sharply lower simply because it will take longer until their cash flows become significant.

Moral of the story: You cannot successfully invest in growth stocks without correctly analyzing where the business cycle is now and where it is going in the near future. There is a time to buy and ride aggressive-growth stocks and a time not to. In a growing economy, hypergrowth stocks tend to outperform other stocks because they have the economic wind at their back, which creates the discretionary capital budgets—the fuel—to meet and exceed lofty earnings growth expectations.

In periods of contracting growth, the opposite occurs in most cases. Economically sensitive stocks fail to meet growth expectations because they have the economic winds in their face. In times of economic contraction, there is not enough excess cash available to let corporations and consumers fund the strategic but discretionary productivity-enhancing investments they so readily make in times of economic growth.

Bottom line: If you want to learn how to profitably ride the world's fastest waves of transformational change, you are going to have to learn how to recognize the signs of changing economic growth patterns. Don't worry, it's a lot easier than you think.

MARKETQUAKES: FORECASTING THE BUSINESS CYCLE IN JUST 10 MINUTES A WEEK

I'm not a big fan of most economists. In the last 20 years that I've been an investor or investment manager, I've found only a handful who have been able to forecast future economic growth accurately. Most economists forecasting the business cycle make the mistake of focusing on esoteric financial minutiae that have little or no relevance to the real economy.

But over the years I've also found a few economists who consistently get it right and keep it very simple. Their research led me to focus on just two indicators to accurately forecast future economic strength or weakness of the business cycle: the interest rate yield curve and monthly unemployment rates. You can follow these indicators in 10 minutes a week or less.

When these two powerful forecasting tools signal a change in the economy, I call it a "MarketQuake," because more often than not an earthquake-like shift lies ahead for the economy, the business cycle, and the stock market. ChangeWave investors use these two simple MarketQuake signals to forecast future economic strength or weakness— and we adjust our portfolio mix of ballast-growth and aggressive-/speculative-growth stocks accordingly.

THE YIELD CURVE: YOUR KEY TO FORECASTING ECONOMIC GROWTH

I know that the idea of a "positive" or "inverted" yield curve (that is, the difference in yield between the three-month Treasury bill and the 10-year Treasury note) is enough to make most investors roll their eyes. But if I told you that over the last 100 years whenever a simple graph of the differential in their respective current yields sloped positive a period of economic growth would result, it might get your attention. (This occurs when you get a higher yield for the longer-dated bonds than for the shorter-term bonds.)

Welcome to the yield curve. You are now an economic forecaster.

Inversion . . . and Reversion: Yield Spread Between Three-Month Treasury and Ten-Year Treasury

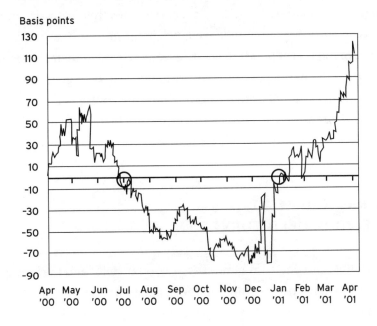

Source: Baseline

Furthermore, if you knew that when this yield curve inverted—that is, when *short-term* bonds delivered a higher yield than long-term bonds—the odds of an oncoming recession were 90%, I think you'd find the yield curve a little sexier.

The fact is that for most of 2000, the bond market was clearly signaling that the economy was quickly headed for a significant slowdown, but no one listened. In fact, an obscure 1996 report by the Fed concluded that the yield curve was the most accurate indicator of future economic growth and decline after testing hundreds of more esoteric and complicated models.

Simply stated, an upward-sloping or positive yield curve means that investors accept lower yields on shorter-term bonds, which in turn means the bond market is forecasting better times ahead. Why?

Naturally, one would expect that an investor assumes more economic risk (and more reward) on longer-dated bonds since there is more uncertainty about what might happen 10 years down the road than in the next three months. Thus, when short-term bond maturities yield less than longer-term bonds (that is, the yield curve is positively sloped), investors are saying that they are confident enough in the future to assume the higher risk of long-term bonds to get the greater reward of their higher yield.

When the differential in short-to-long bond yield goes negative, or the slope of the graph is said to *invert*, it means investors are demanding higher yields for short-term debt. In other words, they feel there is greater risk coming in the months ahead than, say, in a decade or two.

MARKETQUAKE #1:
THE 2001 YIELD CURVE

When the short end (three-month to two-year yield) and the long end of the yield curve (two-year to 10-year) sloped positive on April 19, 2001, the bond market was telling us that the recession probabilities four quarters ahead were less than 5%, according to the Fed study. Just as it did in late 1998. Conversely, in the first quarter of 1974, 1981, and 2000, the

Estimated Recession Probabilities for
Probit Model Using the Yield Curve Spread

Four Quarters Ahead

Recession Probability (Percent)	Value of Spread (Percentage Points)
5	1.21
10	0.76
15	0.46
20	0.22
25	0.02
30	-0.17
40	-0.50
50	-0.82
60	-1.13
70	-1.46
80	-1.85
90	-2.40

Note: The yield curve spread is defined as the spread between the interest rates on the 10-year Treasury note and the three-month Treasury bill.

yield curve spread averaged –2.18%, signaling an 86.5% recession risk. As predicted, recessions followed.

The lesson? When the yield curve inverts more than –2%, it's time to start making plans to kick off your rapid-growth, high-P/E ChangeWave stocks and load up on ballast-growth-industry stocks—and vice versa. When the yield curve slope is +2% or more, economic growth and expansion is nine to 12 months ahead.

Forecasting hint No. 1: Short-term interest rates generally follow the lead of the Federal Reserve monetary policy. When the Fed starts raising interest rates, you can bet that short-term interest rates are headed higher—and you should be on the lookout for an inverted yield curve within six to nine months of Fed action.

Forecasting hint No. 2: When the Fed starts raising rates, smart investors in aggressive-growth stocks start making plans to take profits and switch ChangeWaves. When the Fed starts to cut rates, we start looking for newly emerging rapid-growth ChangeWaves to ride.

Why Does the Fed Meddle with Short-Term Interest Rates?

A quick lesson in Fed watching: In our modern age, the Federal Reserve's monetary policy is used to speed up or slow down our economy via the cash, or "liquidity," it pours into our monetary system. How much the Fed "stimulates" or suppresses our economic growth is primarily based on its forecast for price inflation.

When the Fed judges that there are too many dollars chasing too few goods and services (i.e., the risk of inflation is higher than the risk of recession), it resorts to the blunt pile-driver approach of economic management. It withdraws liquidity (a.k.a. cash) from our system and raises short-term interest rates until the Fed believes demand for goods and services comes into balance with supply of cash to pay for them. This process, unfortunately, is as much art as science.

You can chart the business cycle fairly accurately by using the S-curve approach to Fed interest rate direction. S-curve–like upturns in interest rates precede economic slowdowns. Reverse S-curve drops in the Fed fund rates precede economic growth bottoms and reversals.

According to the Fed studies, the business cycle contraction historically bottoms nine to 12 months after the Fed begins interest rate cuts and increases monetary stimulus (i.e., adds liquidity to loosen the monetary system). This peaks six to 12 months after the Fed has begun to raise short-term interest rates and tighten monetary policy (i.e., takes cash out of the system).

More simply, when the Fed starts changing its monetary policy, be on guard for a changing economy.

MARKETQUAKE NO. 2:
THE NO-BRAINER RECESSION FORECAST

Knowing when we are in a recession (i.e., the bust period of a business cycle, with significant economy-wide growth contraction) is crucial for any investor. In the twentieth century, the stock market has always rebooted its bull markets well before the recession ended. In 1976, the market actually rallied at the beginning of the recession. But in the 10 recessions since World War II, the stock market has moved significantly higher *well before* the end of each recession.

Since rapid-growth ChangeWaves do better at the beginning and middle of economic expansions, maximizing investment gains means you must begin to take your aggressive- and speculative-growth stock positions when the economic outlook is bleakest—that is, when economic improvement is not yet apparent to most investors.

Once again, economists are no help in deciphering recessions. Recessions are typically declared by the experts six to nine months *after* they occur. My formula is simple and much more timely. What I have found is that when the monthly unemployment statistics say the economy is creating jobs, we are in an expansion. When our economy is not creating jobs, it means our economy is contracting. For purposes of economic forecasting, let's call this period of job destruction what it really is: a recession.

For example, the unemployment rate started indicating that the economy was losing jobs in December 2000. Since the average recession lasts about 10 months, and the market on average starts to rally at the midpoint of a recession (declared or not), this model told ChangeWave investors to continue to emphasize ballast stocks through the spring but anticipate a market rally and, ideally, start switching on to rapid-growth ChangeWaves in the late summer or fall of 2001.

Both of these economic numbers are available in the *Wall Street Journal, Barron's, Business Week,* www.dismalscience.com, and a host of other Web sites.

The "invisible hand" of the Fed takes time to work through our system. But smart investors used the business cycle to work offensive and defensive strategies.

END OF CLASS

When you combine the simple economic forecasting method of the yield curve with the even simpler definition of recession/expansion, you have all the information you need to:

- Jump on the rapid-growth ChangeWaves at the most profitable time in the business cycle—the reexpansion through peak growth phases of the business cycle
- Jump off economically sensitive rapid-growth ChangeWaves to start building dominant allocation in ballast-growth ChangeWaves
- Keep your growth portfolio growing in expanding and recessionary economies

CHAPTER TEN

Selecting the Right Spaces

Now that you know when it's safe to ride the two kinds of ChangeWaves, you still need a way to cut your ChangeWaves and sweet-spot spaces to a manageable shortlist.

This is where we use the ChangeWave Scorecard to separate the good investment opportunities from the great ones. In ChangeWave Investing we grade the investment potential of our space leaders by an objective space ranking and rating strategy.

We start with your investment premise—the primary reason why you think that particular space and particular stock is going to be worth more than the price you paid for it. Without a premise, you don't have an investment—you just own a stock.

More than anything else, what ChangeWave Investing does to dramatically improve your investing success is to help you develop rock-solid investment premises. The quality of your investment premise-building makes a huge difference between you and most other investors.

Remember, when someone tells you "this is a great stock," remind them that there are no great stocks. There are only great companies with enormous profit opportunities because they lead and address huge and rapidly growing addressable market spaces superior to 99% of the world's other business opportunities.

The job of ChangeWave investment premise-building is to lead you to own the great stocks of the world's great growth industries and know exactly why you own them. The development of rock-hard conviction about *what* you own and *why* you own it will serve you incredibly well, as you'll soon see.

CONTEXT FIRST, MONEY SECOND

To build a great investment premise you have to put it in the context of other opportunities for investment. This means screening away 95% to 99% of potential investment areas to focus *only* on the industrial areas most likely to launch monster ChangeWaves.

We do this by first limiting the rapid-growth ChangeWaves we look to ride to ones occurring in the Techonomy food chain (the only exception I make to this rule are regulatory-based ChangeWaves or individual corporate strategic ChangeWaves that meet my earnings growth criteria). With the Techonomy industries projected to average at least three times the average annual growth rates of non-Techonomy industries over the next 10 to 20 years, this first screen for finding the most investable ChangeWaves is a true no-brainer.

This first cut alone eliminates 80% of the companies and industries in the world and gets our universe of potential ChangeQuakes and Change-Waves down to a reasonable size.

Next we discriminate by revenue growth.

HOW DO YOU GET THE GROWTH FORECAST
RESEARCH ON THESE CHANGEWAVES?

You don't have to do this research on your own—use existing industry consultant studies you find in your wave mapping to get these forecasts. Search on the names of consultants you've found that follow the space you are researching.

For example, the gigabit Ethernet ChangeWave represents the transition to a gigabit Ethernet market from the old "10/100T" technology. The ChangeQuake that launched the wave was a new chip design standard from companies like Marvell Technology Group (MRVL) that allowed companies to upgrade the speed of their local area networks by a factor of more than 600 times over old T-1 rates without ripping out old phone lines—a definite killer value proposition.

Search the word "gigabit Ethernet" on my favorite search engine, google.com, and you find the Del'Oro Group. They are projecting sales of gigabit Ethernet switches to grow from $2.5 billion to $10.5 billion. Cahner's In-Stat Group, another consultant in the field, looks for growth from $3.7 billion in 2000 to $17 billion in 2004.

Take the average 2004 sales ($10.5B + $17B = $27.5B ÷ 2) and you get $13.75 billion. Subtract from the average starting market size ($2.5B + $3.7B) ÷ 2, or $3.1 billion, and you get a $10.65 billion difference.

Divide by average of the growth over four years (2000 to 2004), and you have a simple average ChangeWave annual growth rate of more than $2.6 billion—clearly a ChangeWave meeting our discrimination strategy.

ADDRESSED THREE- TO FIVE-YEAR
MARKET OPPORTUNITY

In this example, the forecastable addressed market opportunity—the amount of forecasted annual spending on gigabit Ethernet switching in

2004—is $13.75 billion. The idea here is that all things being equal, a ChangeWave growing 50% a year from 2001 to 2004 with annual sales of $10 billion is a much more fertile ground for finding monster stocks than one growing the same rate but only to $1 billion in annual sales.

A great example of a ChangeWave rich in lucrative subsectors or spaces is the ChangeWave to storage area networking from traditional network storage.

A storage area network (SAN) is a special network of storage devices, connected with a special networking technology called fiber channel, whose killer value proposition to the traditional network storage solution is 100-plus times lower cost of data storage for data-storage-intensive enterprises. The SAN ChangeWave compound annual growth rate (CAGR) is more than 95% through 2003, with an addressed market opportunity of more than $27 billion.

The SAN ChangeWave wave map is composed of three subsector spaces: (1) the storage devices themselves, (2) the fiber channel host bus adapters (HBAs), and (3) hubs and switches.

The SAN storage device business itself is growing by more than 100% a year, the HBA industry by more than 60%, and the hub/switch space by more than 125% on a projected annualized basis.

The storage area network ChangeWave continues to be a rich source of very hot spaces and space-leading stocks.

NEXT CUT IS SPACE DISCRIMINATION: THE 25%/$1 BILLION RULE

Investing is a very direct, skilled, and legitimate form of discrimination. In ChangeWave growth investing, we discriminate against our Techonomy market spaces within the leading ChangeWaves by rate of growth and addressed market size.

In ChangeWave Investing, we are looking to generate at least 25% annual returns on our portfolio of growth stocks. Thus, to achieve this goal (without the benefit of another stock market bubble), we need stocks that can grow their businesses (and earnings) by *at least* 25% a year.

We limit our ChangeWave research to those emerged industrial sub-sectors or spaces projected to grow by at least 25% a year over the next three to five years. This growth rate hurdle gives you the best chance of finding companies that will exceed 25% annual appreciation.

We also look for spaces that will grow to at least $1 billion in revenues within the initial three- to five-year forecastable period. Monster stocks come from monster opportunities—the bigger the end market, the bigger the market-leading stocks can be.

For newly emerging speculative growth ChangeWaves, I suggest you make the cut at 50%-plus annual growth for the three- to five-year forecastable future. But *100%-plus projected growth* is what you are really looking for.

For individual company Strategic ChangeWaves, use a minimum 25% average earnings-per-share growth rate year-over-year from the strategic ChangeQuake and look for companies with a minimum of $100 million in sales. I find that smaller companies don't have the depth of management to execute strategic shifts very well.

AVERAGE GROSS MARGIN

How much does the average player in the space earn from every product or service sold? Our criterion is a minimum of 50% gross margin from every sale. Our average Techonomy space in infotech (especially software) usually delivers more than 60% gross margin per sale. Gross margin is the measurement of how much it costs to make or deliver a service before corporate overhead and other indirect costs are subtracted from each sale. How much does the company make from every sale minus cost of goods sold?

This measurement or metric is the biggest space killer of all time. Using this single criterion kept us out of huge fast-growing spaces that ultimately bombed in the Internet stock bubble like e-retailing, server storage, e-consulting, and others.

You can get gross margin numbers from most investment research databases available on the Web—in places like Yahoo and www.Market-guide.com.

THE CHANGEWAVE SCORECARD

Once you have mapped a few highly rated ChangeWaves, you come up with eight to ten equally measured exciting spaces. Rank your favorite spaces by the following measures:

- **Forecastable Compound Annual Growth Rate (CAGR).** How fast we can expect the industry or company to grow its earnings over the next three to five years?
- **Addressed Market Opportunity.** How big will the annual revenue in the industry be in three to five years?
- **Average Gross Margin.** How much does the industry make from every sale minus cost of goods sold?

You come up with a small but powerful universe of spaces from which to build yourself an eight to 10-stock aggressive-growth ChangeWave portfolio.

Rank your spaces from highest to lowest. The space with the lowest score wins. That means the space that ranks highest in all three categories earns the fewest points—that's good!

FINAL THOUGHT: INVESTING IS INTELLIGENT DISCRIMINATION

In life, discrimination is wrong and unfair. As far as investing goes, fair is a weather report. Intelligent discrimination is the most basic component of growth-investing success.

Being your own growth investment portfolio manager is like being captain of a pickup basketball team where you get to choose whomever you want to be on your team. If your goal is to win (and listen—if building a winning portfolio and beating the returns that market index investors get is *not* your goal, then you are reading the wrong book), whom would you rather pick for your team—Michael Jordan or Michael Bolton? Vince Carter or Vince McMahon?

For example, you may love books—I know I do. But do I own book publishing companies in my aggressive-growth portfolio? Absolutely not—they don't even meet one of our discrimination criteria.

ChangeWave Investing Thesis No. 5:
All premises are not born equal. Don't let your love of a company
or industry cloud your discriminatory fervor.

The ChangeWave fundamental screening process cuts your candidates for your team "draft" down to the most attractive growth spaces and the primary beneficiaries of that growth. By the time you have selected ChangeWaves and their hottest spaces, you will have cut 99% of the industries and 99.9% of available public companies from your "draft universe."

Now you are ready to make some money.

PART THREE

Making Money in ChangeWave Stocks

CHAPTER ELEVEN

ChangeWave Investing

OK—you are now an official change analyst. You know how to distinguish investable changes and how to analyze the investable change food chain to identify the most likely beneficiaries. You know that "the right stock in the best space wins" means the market-share leader/coleader in the fastest sustainable growth industry earning the highest gross profit margins is the odds-on favorite to become a stock market winner in a growing overall economy.

You are like the hard-core surfer who became an amateur weatherman in order to anticipate where the best waves will be breaking. You also have learned to perform your own economic forecasting to anticipate upcoming periods of economic growth and contraction. That also helps you choose the rapid-growth or ballast-growth ChangeWaves most likely to benefit from the boom-to-bust business cycle.

So now the $64 million question: When do *you* buy your favored stock? When do *you* sell it? How do you know when it's fairly valued? Why do some stocks get valued at significant premiums to the average stock? Why do others consistently sell at a discount to the norm?

To answer these questions, a little more training is required. At this stage you are like a kid with a new driver's license about to take delivery of a Ferrari. Now you've got to understand the environment you are going to be driving in. The risks. The unwritten rules.

Most important, you can do all this yourself. You are not dependent on advice from Wall Street that you most likely would never get anyway. Too harsh? Has your broker ever called you to *sell* a winning stock?

THE BASIC CHANGEWAVE GAME: PICK THE ULTIMATE LEADER

In every ChangeWave space we invest in, our ultimate strategy is to invest in and hold the company that starts out an emerging leader of a soon-to-be multibillion-dollar space and grows to become what we call the "Game-Over Dominator." (This is for reasons we will point out in a minute.) These are the ultimate monster sweet-spot space investments—like Cisco, Solectron, Intel, and Microsoft—that turn $10,000 investments into million-dollar portfolios.

The way aggressive investors get rapidly and radically rich in Change-Wave Investing is to find a great ChangeWave sweet spot and invest in the company that, in turn, becomes the Game-Over Dominator of that space.

When you ride a company from emerging leadership to Game-Over Dominator status in an emerging space that grows into a $10-billion-plus-a-year industry, you have won the game. And you have built a not-so-small fortune in the process.

There are three types of leading companies you'll find in any Change-Wave industrial space (ranked by lowest to highest investment risk):

Game-Over Dominators. The companies whose market-share leadership of their space is too strong to be vanquished. In information technology spaces, this company has become the industry standard or natural monopoly.

Emerged Leader. The company that has taken the market-share lead and is growing it toward domination, but all-out victory cannot be claimed.

Emerging Leader. The space that has two or three leaders with more than 15% market share who are fighting it out in a death match.

Everybody Else. These are the companies (including non–pure plays) that we screen out and do not bother with.

Once you have found one or more sweet-spot spaces that meet your criteria for investment opportunity, the whole point in ChangeWave Investing is to ride the top emerging leaders until one becomes the emerged or game-over leader. When a clear leader emerges, we sell the laggards and hold on to the market-share leader until the rapid-growth phase of the ChangeWave begins to crest. (Remember, that's when the S-curve reaches demand saturation and begins to flatten.) Now it's time to sell our winning stock and move on the new waves.

For example, I rode Microsoft (MSFT), Dell (DELL), and Intel for much of the '90s. Their growth was unbelievable—each one up more than 2,000% during their growth periods. But as the PC ChangeWave S-curve started to tail in late 1999 and early 2000, I jumped off. I jumped off Cisco in the summer of 2000 for the same reason—flattening, saturated demand in the enterprise networking space.

But while these companies were leading their respective Change-Waves, they were great rides. They created billions of dollars of wealth for their investors, and changed the financial lives of every investor who owned their stock.

However, only the investors who converted those gains into real cash actually made real money.

What Makes ChangeWave Sweet-Spot Leading Companies So Darn Valuable?

What made them go up so much? Why do industry leaders grow to such enormous valuations while the other competitors do not? Why did I sell

Cisco, Dell, and Microsoft when all the experts said they were still great stocks? Why did Microsoft, Intel, Dell, and Cisco drop more than 60% to 80% in value during 2000–2001, giving back more than *$1 trillion* in market value?

To answer these questions, it's time to talk about the stock market. You see, your understanding of how to find and how to ride Change-Waves is invaluable. You know more about growth investing than do 99% of all investors.

Unfortunately, however, until you get a firm grasp on the basic logic of the stock market, you will not make the fortune you desire.

What Makes Stocks Go Up and Down?

In the long run, share prices track earnings growth. In the short run, stocks move up and down on pure greed and fear. In perhaps the most abstract view, it is the degree of current optimism or pessimism over a company's future earnings potential (relative to those of similar companies) compounded by the prevailing emotions of greed and fear that fuel or dampen the rise and fall of stock prices.

In the least abstract view, however, what makes a stock go up or down is simply the balance of available inventory of the stock for sale at any one moment (supply) and the number of investors who want to own the stock (demand). When a stock goes up, there is a positive supply/demand imbalance—more people who want to buy shares at the current price than there are shares available for sale. To loosen up shares for sale, eager buyers bid higher prices.

The opposite occurs, of course, when the price of a stock goes down.

When there are more stockholders wanting to buy and hold a stock than stockholders wanting to sell a stock, the stock continues to go up in price because inventory of stock for sale becomes smaller and smaller. In other words, the supply/demand imbalance grows *more* acute—as more investors buy and hold a stock, they reduce the inventory available for sale. This leads stock owners to ask ever-higher prices for their stock until demand for the stock becomes less than the supply of willing sellers.

The key idea here is that there is a direct correlation between the amount of stock (inventory) for sale every day and the ownership duration of existing stockholders. A stock has a bull market when its shares are held by more investors who intend to keep the stock for a long time than by investors who want to own it for only a short time.

In the daily open auction called the stock market, stock prices are the ultimate proof of the economic laws of supply and demand.

At some price, however, some long-term stockholders can't resist the price that the stock has reached and they agree to sell. When more inventory of stock comes on the market at a price higher than buyers are willing to pay, the inventory of stock is considered to be negatively out-of-balance and asking price of the stock is lowered until a willing buyer steps in. The balance of available supply and willing buyers has reversed. Now there are more willing sellers than willing buyers and prices must be lowered until a willing buyer steps in and bids for the stock.

If the stock is sold to long-term investors, these "price corrections" are temporary and work themselves out in a few weeks. The stock eventually resumes its positive supply/demand imbalance—that is, the stock price stabilizes and starts to creep back to its previous value. If, however, the new buyers are short-term buyers, the stock price will become highly volatile as a transfer of *ownership intent* takes place.

In pure supply/demand terms, this is the essence of what a bear market is for a stock or the market as a whole. Previously strong, high-conviction stock ownership becomes weak, low-conviction ownership. When strong-conviction ownership turns weak, stock prices go down.

The bear market for a stock ends when this rotation comes full circle—that is, the negative imbalance reverses. The weak ownership has rotated to strong, high-conviction ownership, and the strong, high-conviction ownership again changes to inventory supply dynamics.

A bottom is reached in a market or a stock itself when a fundamental shift in stock ownership psychology (high-conviction versus low-conviction stockholders) occurs. You know this has happened when people are willing to sell only on an uptick to a buyer willing to pay more, not on a downtick at any price and to anybody willing to pay anything.

So What Creates High-Conviction Stockholders?

Confidence. Confidence in the future earnings growth rate of the industry, confidence in the company's ability to capitalize on its opportunity, and confidence in the continued inflation-controlled growth rate of the economy as a whole.

Economic lecture time again. In free-market capitalism, growth investment capital moves for essentially three reasons:

- It moves *toward* the most predictable secular growth opportunity and beneficiary.
- It moves *away* from the reverse—predictable slowing growth and its predictable casualty or victim.
- Last but not least, investment capital moves because someone believable is doing a good job of selling a stock's growth story. On Wall Street that's called "sponsorship." You must never forget that stocks are, in reality, no different from any other product or service. They need to be merchandised and sold or they sit on the shelf without selling until they are drastically discounted.

You may find it helpful to think of the stock market like this: It's simply a daily worldwide economic pessimism or optimism voting machine. Every day, people vote with their investment capital on how optimistic or pessimistic their conviction is toward future economic growth of the economy and an individual company's chances to exceed the economy's average rate of growth.

What Turns Regular Stocks into Monster Stocks?

If stocks need high-conviction stockholders to keep their inventory supply in "positive imbalance," where do these high-conviction stockholders come from? How can one stock go up thousands of percentage points in a year (i.e., attract thousands of highly convicted stockholders), while other stocks go nowhere?

Again, in the long run, it's the company's ability to consistently grow its profitability ever higher. But the behavioral answer lies in the innate buying behavior that is hardwired into the minds and personalities of tens of millions of potential stockbuyers.

You undoubtedly have heard of the popular concept of adoption curves, or product life cycles. It's where the term "early adopter" comes from. The concept is that you can group people into subsets based on where they tend to land on the "adoption curve" for new products or services. Years of testing led social scientists to conclude that your position on this adoption curve is mostly hardwired into your personality. It is this hardwiring that makes the behavior repeatable and measurable.

From earliest to latest adopters, these groups are called:

The Innovators. These people are the earliest to welcome and adapt to new things—the bleeding edge. Innovators make up about 3% to 5% of the world.

The Early Adopters. This group represents the next 10% to 15% of adopters. Not bleeding edge, but leading edge.

The Early Majority. These are the early pragmatists who say, "I need solid evidence (and peer pressure from the early adopters) before I act." They make up about 34% of the world.

The Late Majority. This is the "I need conclusive evidence to buy" crowd (who also need peer pressure from the early majority). Another 34%.

The Laggards/Nonadopters. Enough said.

How does this relate to stock buying and selling? People buy stocks the same way they buy other products. The same predictable behavior that causes people to buy new products carries over to stocks.

When an emerging space coleader stock executes on its business plan well enough to move from the leadership pack to the Game-Over Dominator position, it attracts different investor types along the way.

Think of each group as having a finite amount of cash to spend on stocks. What makes a stock skyrocket is when the stock's story is adopted by the Early and Late Majority investors. That's because they (on a pure percentage basis) have the most money.

Innovator and Early Adopter money tends to buy a stock during the foundational phase of the S-curve. They raise the stock 100% or so. But it's the big money of the Early and Late Adopter cash that really skyrockets the stock and continues the supply imbalance that raises stock bids ever higher.

To keep the high-conviction stockholders in the majority, it matters *what type* of stockholders eventually own the stock, too.

THE THREE TYPES OF AGGRESSIVE-GROWTH PLAYERS: THE FRONT, MIDDLE, AND REAR GUARD

Who are these investors? There are three types of investors that play the aggressive stock investing game. The first and most important group is the fundamental owners, and in the end, stock prices maintain their upward path because there are more high-conviction fundamental owners than the other two types of investors. Let me explain.

Fundamental investors care first, last, and only about the underlying strength of the industry space and the individual company's underlying business. In particular, the fundamental analyst is concerned almost totally with determining the size and growth rate of a company's future earnings.

Why the earnings fixation? Let's step back for another quick dab of investment theory. Any given security (stock, bonds, options, etc.) theoretically has an intrinsic value—defined as the sum of all future cash flows that the security will provide over its life, adjusted (or "discounted") to today at the prevailing interest rate relative to the future years of cash flow being discounted.

The fundamental analysis game for growth investors is to figure out which stocks are best able to reach and achieve superior earnings growth rates and thus earn and maintain premium-to-market valuations. If the market price is significantly below their present-day intrinsic valuation calculation, the stock is undervalued and can be profitably bought.

Aggressive fundamental growth investors are Innovator and Early

Adopter investors. They make their money being early and right. With direct and indirect analysis, they form their investment thesis as to why they think a particular stock or sector of stocks will out-earn the market averages. They tend to buy stocks long (i.e., betting they will go up in value) and hold their positions the longest.

Stocks depend on fundamental stockholders to maintain their value during times of correction and bear markets. Fundamental buyers are the high-conviction stockholders that low-conviction sellers sell to during normal market corrections.

The Technical Analysts

Fundamental analysis involves lots of work but often is wrong and thus adds little incremental value to the stock-picking game. Many investors feel that the whole fundamental game is pointless. They argue that the market is so efficient (i.e., securities prices reflect new information so quickly) that no investor can gain any information that would provide a meaningful advantage.

In this camp are the technical analysts and traders, who study and analyze stock-trading patterns. The "TA" crowd uses bar charts and graphs of stock-price movements and trading-volume patterns to decide which stocks are poised to move up or down more than others. The TA camp includes mostly Early Majority and Late Adopter investors. Many technicians do look to fundamentals after they have spotted a stock that is exhibiting patterns they like. But they believe first in the recurring behavioral power of human nature and the recurring nature of specific stock-movement patterns. It is their main criterion for forming their buy/sell/hold judgments.

True TA investors believe that all information pertinent to a stock's future earnings and future growth is reflected in the company's past market prices and volume. In other words, they believe fundamental analysis is a complete waste of time.

They only buy stocks long (i.e., bet that a stock price will rise), with uptrending charts showing above-market average upward strength.

Upward trends mean that the demand part of the inventory equation is in control—there are more people who want to buy than people who are willing to sell. They short stocks (bet the price goes down) when stocks look unusually weak to them—i.e., the stock-trend downward slope means that supply is in control.

Their basic strategic logic is simple handicapping—making an educated guess as to the future perceptions of other investors based on the trends of the stock's day-to-day pricing and volume. As the famous economist and incredibly successful investor John Maynard Keynes said when asked about his secret, "If you're going to bet on who's going to win a beauty contest, don't bet on who you think is most beautiful, but who you believe the judges think is most beautiful."

Buying a stock based on a powerful uptrend is a bet that investors will continue to find that stock attractive.

Long-term technical investors are healthy for a stock as long as it maintains a positive technical trend line. Technical investors can be high-conviction stockholders as long as the chart of the stock looks beautiful to them. They become a *liability* to the stock when the chart breaks down and turns ugly. They want to own only technically beautiful stocks.

A Once-Beautiful Chart—EMC

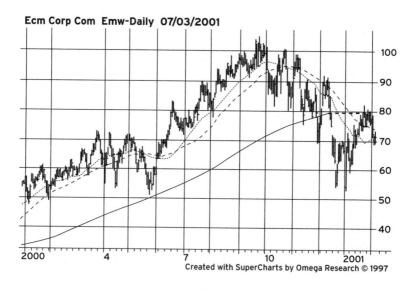

Ecm Corp Com Emw-Daily 07/03/2001

Created with SuperCharts by Omega Research © 1997

The Momo Investors

The last guys are the momentum investors. I call them "Momos."

Momos are Late Majority stock adopters. Beauty to them means positive, increasing price and earnings momentum—stocks with a trend line of higher earnings and higher prices. They usually subscribe to a form of Newtonian physics that holds that "a beautiful stock is one that is in an upward motion because it tends to stay in that upward motion—until it doesn't." When the upward movement stops, or the positive earnings growth slows, momentum investors sell immediately.

When you see a stock moving up more than double the rate of the market as a whole, the momentum investors are more than likely responsible.

The point to remember here is that when *any* of your growth stocks start moving 5% to 10% a day, your stock is being bought by momentum buyers. When your stock gets caught up in this trading whirlwind, you are going to have to make a hold or sell decision within weeks—even days.

Momentum investors are the answer to how a stock can go from $5 to $100 in a three-month period. Their all-or-nothing investment style is self-fulfilling. Because Momos are buying, the stock imbalance is positive

The Momo's Strike MicroStrategy

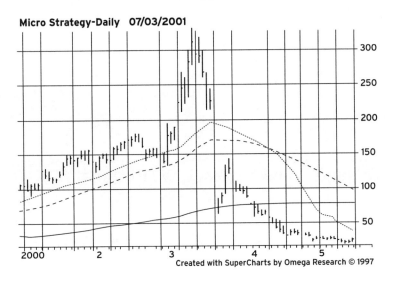

Micro Strategy-Daily 07/03/2001

Created with SuperCharts by Omega Research © 1997

and the buy price is bid up. Because the price is being bid up, more Momos are attracted to the stock, so it's bid higher. This is called a melt-up. Here the buyer-to-seller imbalance is so strong that there are 5-to-1 or 10-to-1 buy orders for every share offered for sale.

When your stock's chart starts looking like this (see chart on page 129), your high conviction about your stock is going to get tested because the price is being set up for a big, big reverse price correction. Not if—when. One day, some negative fundamental or industry news item will hit and the stock the Momos were buying will go down.

Now "reverse momentum" occurs. You have a stock meltdown. When a stock you own enters what I call the "Momo zone," you know it is only a matter of time before your gloriously profitable melt-up turns to a meltdown. Meltdowns follow melt-ups 100% of the time. They follow the same rules of S-curve transformations. When a melt-up reaches a saturation point and everyone who would buy has bought—*boom*—the demand imbalance turns into a supply surplus imbalance in the blink of an eye. And your stock crumbles 30% to 50% or more in value as the Momos rush for the exits while long-term investors watch in shock.

We'll talk about how to handle this situation to make enormous profits later, but now you have the whole picture. My point is that the type of stockholders who buy your favorite ChangeWave stock determine the short-term and long-term future of its pricing. Monster stocks attract all three types of stockholders.

To keep its stock price high for years rather than months, however, your growth stock is going to have to continue to attract high-conviction, fundamental-driven stockholders. This means you need to understand how *they* value stocks.

AGGRESSIVE-GROWTH STOCK VALUATIONS

Most institutional fundamental-based investment managers, as part of their stock-picking evidence, try to figure out what a stock is going to be worth a year or two after they buy it. These future stock valuations come down roughly to the same formula. Here it is: The future price of the stock is equal to the forecasted amount of future earnings or revenue of the company times a projected future price-to-earnings ratio. (That means the multiple investors figure others will pay in the future for what they perceive to be the company's future earnings.)

The higher the P/E ratio investors think will be paid in the future, the higher the value of the stock today.

For growth stocks, four factors combine to determine the future P/E calculation:

- The rate of earnings growth
- The perceived consistency of earnings growth
- The "excitement factor" of the space
- The "excitement factor" of the company

Sweet-spot spaces riding massive secular ChangeWaves are almost always the most exciting spaces. But the excitement factor for a company is primarily based on the company's apparent sustainable competitive advantage and how likely it can be parlayed into domination of a vast, rapidly expanding secular growth industry.

When Wall Street can make an argument that a company has the competitive edge to become the dominant company (i.e., it's an odds-on Game-Over Dominator) in a long-term, rapid-growth industry, it gets very excited. The simplest and most compelling logic of this argument comes when a company is growing its market share more than 15% per year and/or growing its profit margin faster than its competitors and faster than most other industries.

The logic here is simple: The only kind of company that can deliver this kind of financial performance is one with a locked-in advantage over its competitors. It has to have something the marketplace wants and needs that other providers cannot easily replicate or deliver. Thus, in Wall Street's eyes, evaluation of sustainable competitive advantage is the main event in judging the Wall Street beauty contest—that is, which stocks will be considered most attractive. Evaluating a company's competitive advantage and its sustainability, ahead of Wall Street, is a crucial puzzle to solve.

COMPETITIVE ADVANTAGE

Let's focus on Economics 101 for a second. Competitive advantage in a free and open marketplace is ultimately derived from providing better value for equivalent cost to a market of customers (better known as the "strategic differentiation control point" to marketers) or equivalent customer value for a meaningful lower cost ("a low-cost-provider strategic control point").

Fundamental securities analysts look to the strategic control points, because in a fast-growing space, the greater a company's strategic control over its customers, the greater the predictability of its earnings growth. The most valuable strategic control points a company can possess, New Economy or Old Economy, are built-in barriers for their customers to switch to competitive alternatives.

Management theorist Peter Drucker said that, for a product or service to be adopted readily by consumers, it needs to be perceived as having 10 times the value of its predecessor.

In the agrarian economy, land and resources determined who won and who lost. Michael Porter, the eminent Harvard business strategy professor, teaches that controlling the value chain in the industrial economy is the basis of competition. In the industrial age, the company that most controls its value chain wins.

In our emerging Techonomy, where knowledge, information, and the replacement of labor for capital are emerging as the currencies of competition, strategic control points have become intangible assets. These include databases, brands, copyrights, two-year development leadership, and even unique organizational design or hard-to-replicate business model design.

According to Alberto Vilar, a leading investor in emerging tech, there are several key determinants of "beauty" in an emerging tech stock:

- The transformational power of the technology intellectual property (patents and lead time)
- The potential size of the new markets created

- The ability of management to execute
- The profitability of the business model

To Mr. Vilar's list I would, of course, add:

- The size and growth magnitude of the ChangeWave it's riding
- The size and growth magnitude of the space the company's competing in
- The sweet-spot positioning of the space within its ChangeWave(s)

Since the value of companies is increasingly enhanced by their intangible assets, ChangeWave investors looking for emerging-space leaders will have to judge the value of a company as *a strategic aggregation of intangible assets*, as well as by how well these assets are used to create a competitive advantage within the world's fastest-growing new marketplaces.

When you find a company able to create and sustain a competitive advantage in a rapidly growing sector of our economy, you have found the massive compound earnings growth machine we call the Game-Over Dominator. More often than not, this company will be accorded a premium-to-market P/E multiple, and will deserve its premium valuation.

MAKE DUST OR EAT DUST

There is another factor at work that skews premium valuations to certain companies. Steve Smith of Broadview Associates (a leading tech merger and acquisition house) calls this the "Make Dust or Eat Dust" factor. Says Smith, "We favor companies that are aggressively acquiring more companies than their competitors. In the investment world we live in, premium market cap valuations go to this 'Alpha Male leader' who outpaces their competitors in getting to game-over dominant size the fastest."

The basic issue here is that people on Wall Street with the most money favor big and liquid stocks. Why? Because liquid stocks (i.e., those that trade millions of shares a day with market valuations exceeding $10 billion) are those that a money manager can get in and out of without taking the stock value apart. Again we are talking inventory here. If money managers turn positive inventory imbalance into negative supply imbalance by putting a million shares up for sale, they can't risk owning the stock. In other words, an institutional investor who can't get out won't get in. So float (the amount of shares available in the open market) and trading volume (liquidity) are key elements to sustainable market caps.

This creates a catch-22 for small- and midcap stocks (under $10 billion market caps) that want to add market value for their stockholders. According to Smith, the fact of the matter is that they have four choices:

1. Be the game-over dominant gorilla
2. Buy in an attempt to become the Game-Over Dominator
3. Sell to the Game-Over Dominator
4. Sell to someone

A fact of life in the Nasdaq (where most technology stocks trade) is that 88% of the trading volume occurs in the game-over dominant big-cap stocks (more than $15 billion to $20 billion market capitalization).

So when looking for emerged leaders who can grow into Game-Over Dominators, look for companies that have an acquisitive nature, like JDS Uniphase (which grew its market cap from $756 million to *$39.36 billion* before it imploded in 2001). Cisco was our poster child of this get-big-or-go-home strategy for years.

In most every case, emerging leaders grow to the emerged and Game-Over Dominator position only by buying their way to the top. Wall Street knows this and pays premium valuations for wanna-be Game-Over Dominator companies who walk the Game-Over-Dominator walk.

CHAPTER TWELVE

What Creates Value in the Techonomy?

A big part of the ChangeWave Investing philosophy is our perception of what value really means in the context of the Techonomy. Traditional value investing involves buying stocks with misunderstood financial or physical-based assets and waiting for the rest of the world to come to understand their true earnings power. This is not what ChangeWave Investing is about.

Trying to outguess 7,000 analysts driven by huge investment banking fees who fight it out every day to earn average market returns in companies like Philip Morris, Alcoa, and International Paper is not the way to realize monster stock gains.

But I do believe that the practice of ChangeWave Investing is a modern form of "value" investing. Stay with me on this one. To my way of thinking, our sweet-spot space leader approach to stock selection is taking advantage of the misunderstood nature and earnings power of *intangible-asset-based* and *knowledge-capital-based* industries and companies. These are the companies that invest in and develop patented and copyrighted intellectual property, knowledge processing, and information assets and leverage them into high-priced, high-profit-margin proprietary products and services. In other words, these are companies that take knowledge capital and intangible assets and turn them into competitive advantage.

HOW A COMPANY IS MISUNDERSTOOD

Let's take the great value investor Sanford Bernstein's description of his approach to value investing as described in his spring 1999 client newsletter: "It's not how good a company is that counts most. It's how misunderstood a company is that counts most. A company does not have to be outstanding for its stock to outperform; it needs to be better than people think it is."

Virtually everyone from the financial and management sides agrees that valuing intangible assets is the most misunderstood part of investing. In that sense, investing in the fastest-growing, intangible-asset-based companies *before* the investment world comes to a common understanding on how to value intangible assets is a modern form of traditional value investing.

VALUE INVESTING THE CHANGEWAVE WAY

In the ChangeWave hybrid form of value investing, we simply ratchet up our wealth-building odds by specializing in industries and market spaces projected to grow at least five to 10 times the average physical asset industry growth rate in times of economic expansion. The companies in our Techonomy spaces are growing their earnings and sales at least 10 to 20 times the rates of growth of industrial-age industries where most "value stocks" live.

What about dividends? some will say. My answer is to forget about paying taxable dividends—growth investors want capital gains. I invest to reap the benefits of one of the last great American tax shelters left to private investors: the ability to sell a radically appreciated stock and pay an 18% capital gains tax on *my* profits.

Why don't we screen for stocks on traditional fundamentals like P/Es, EBITDA (earnings before interest, tax, depreciation, and amortization), and other Old Economy metrics when we are looking for emerging industry leaders? Because in the revolutionary worlds of explosive emerging growth markets, historic standards of analytical economic measurement, or "metrics," plain don't work.

As Alberto Vilar says about his four determinants of emerging technology company success, "Obviously these four questions cannot be answered with much precision at the time of investment in emerging industries." Thus, to expect to invest successfully in emerging technology companies on the standard valuation metrics of price-to-earnings, price-to-sales, price-to-book, et cetera, is patently ridiculous. This is what is fundamentally alien to portfolio managers and analysts who don't specialize in emerging technology investing. These managers who have been trained their entire careers in the traditional Graham-Dodd approach (i.e., discounted cash flow and balance sheet analysis) are at a disadvantage, since Graham-Dodd has no relevance whatsoever to early-stage technology investing.

Bill Miller, the "value" mutual fund manager famous for being the only such manager in America to beat the S&P 500 Index every year of the '90s, tells us, "Traditional valuation metrics, when they work at all, work best with traditional businesses. The value of these traditional analytical tools is usually a function of the historical data supporting their effectiveness. It is true that some of the best technology companies have rarely looked attractive on traditional valuation methods, but that speaks more to the weakness of those methods than to the fundamental risk-reward relationships of those businesses.

"For example, Microsoft (until March 15, 2000) appreciated in value almost 1% a week for 14 years. Companies don't outperform year-in and year-out unless they were radically undervalued (or misunderstood) to begin with."

PROXY VALUATION

Without a set of valuation rules to go by, emerging-growth investors have to come up with a set of measurements or metrics that they feel approximates current valuation reality. In investing, this is called a "proxy valuation" method. This approach allows us to take the massively misunderstood but very real value of a company's intangible assets and come up with an approximate value range. The ChangeWave Investing proxy places a company in context with the size and rate of growth of the fastest secular growth markets in the economy. Then it rates the odds of the company's becoming the dominant "owner" of its space.

In our proxy valuation formula, we figure that the company with the greatest odds of dominating one of the fastest secular growth spaces in the economy possesses the most currently valuable intellectual property on earth.

Thus the ChangeWave Investing process is, in effect, a Techonomy emerging growth-stock valuation tool. It's a proxy method for identifying the stocks most likely to rise in value, based on:

- The size of the addressed market opportunity target
- Their competitive advantage sustainability—that is, the power of their proprietary patented intellectual property to lock in a competitive advantage and other intangible assets
- The proximity of their strategic positioning within the ChangeWave to the sweet spot
- The compound earnings power of their business model as measured by gross margin earned per sale
- Management's ability to execute the business model and turn gross margin into profits
- Their ability and willingness to acquire their way to game-over dominance

In reality, this basic formula of valuing intangible-asset-based companies has validated itself in almost every market space within the information technology industries for the past 20 years.

THE INTANGIBLE ASSET PARADOX

Our bet is that this intangible asset paradox—that is, the disconnect between how valuable intangible assets are versus how they are treated in financial statements—will eventually be solved.

To my thinking, true "value" investing, in the context of emerging Techonomy, means buying companies:

- With the most misunderstood business assets—intangible assets
- In the fastest-growing parts of the economy
- Where their proprietary intellectual property and intangible assets can be leveraged and sold at very high and sustainable gross profit margins to create the most insurmountable competitive advantage and strategic lock-in

When people argue that "the value of a stock is the net present value of its future earnings," I do not disagree at all. I do point out, however, that the other part of the textbook definition of stock valuation is that common stock is also a "call" or share on *all* the assets of a company—both physical and intangible. Since the primary assets of intellectual-property-based companies are not recognized by traditional accounting, I argue that the only place they can be valued is in the security valuation mechanism that we call the public stock market, or in the private market.

My conclusion to the intangible-asset paradox?

The value of a publicly traded stock today, by definition, has to reflect the net present value of the future earnings yield from both the physical and intangible assets of the company. Until the intangible asset paradox is solved, the public market will do its sloppy but better-than-nothing best to value intangible assets.

PRICE-TO-EARNINGS RATIOS IN GROWTH STOCKS

Virtually all investors have at least a vague idea about price-to-earnings ratios—the valuation measurement that relates a stock's valuation premium, or discount, to the overall market by comparing stock price to its earnings per share.

However, most investors' understanding of P/E and high-growth stocks is wrong. The price-to-earnings ratio attempts to be a shorthand for investors to weigh the valuation and appreciation potential of a stock by obtaining the P (current price of the stock) divided by the E (one year's earnings per share). The P/E becomes the "earnings multiple," or the multiple paid for a dollar of earnings from which relative value judgments are made as to various types of companies.

The problem with using P/E ratios to analyze high-growth stocks is that the P/E ratio you get in the paper compares *last year's* earnings per share against the current price. To succeed in high-growth ChangeWave stocks, you have to look *forward* at the earnings potential, as the pros do: You have to come up with a forward P/E ratio that indicates next year's earnings per share. (I'll refer to this as four-quarter forward earnings or consensus forward earnings.)

In my mind, a company's value relative to the overall market is best measured by its *future* prospects, not its past. Many times I find investors saying "ZXW company is too expensive—its P/E is two to three times the average market multiple," when, in fact, relative to the overall market's four-quarter forward earnings growth rate, the stock is currently selling at a *discount!*

Highly rated analyst Mike Kwatinetz, in his book *The Big Tech Score*, captures this concept superbly. To paraphrase Mike, let's take the example of Company A and Company B. They have both finished the past year with $1 of earnings. Company A is an emerging space leader—a high-growth company expected to grow its earnings 100% in the next year. Company B is a leader of a mature business space growing its earnings at 5% a year. If Company A is selling at $50 and Company B is selling at

$25 a share, which stock is the most undervalued? Which one should you buy?

Using last year's P/E ratio, Company A's P/E is 50 and Company B's is 25. Company A's P/E multiple is twice that of B, which means Company A is twice as expensive on a relative basis. That means investors are willing to pay 50 times for $1 earnings and only 25 times $1 of Company B's earnings.

Here is where the forward-looking math answers your investment question. Assuming Company A's earnings are $2 over the next four quarters and Company B's are $1.05, the P/E based on forward earnings would be 25 for Company A and 24 for Company B.

Which is the better buy? On a forward earnings basis they are priced at virtually the same P/E multiple, yet Company A is going to grow its earnings 20 times faster than Company B. Who looks expensive now?

Take these growth rates out three to five years and Company A will deliver you almost $14 of earnings per share versus $1.22 for Company B—in other words, you are paying less than two times today for Company A's earnings per share in year five. If the best 500 companies in the United States grow their forward earnings about 10% a year and sell an average of 25 times their consensus forward earnings, then Company A should be worth 10 to 20 times in the future what you paid today (*if* the growth actually occurs). That's why our ChangeWave analysis pays off.

This is the point of forward-looking P/E ratio analysis. If you're riding one of the fastest-growing ChangeWaves, growing 10 to 20 times faster than the economy as a whole, and your favorite sweet-spot space leader can manage to stay on the wave and deliver on this earnings potential, paying a "premium-to-market P/E multiple" is not only justified— it's imperative. This forward-looking analysis is where strict "value investors" miss out on catching the 1,000% or 10,000% winner stocks, all the while saying these monster stocks are "overvalued."

In ChangeWave Investing, we are trying to buy the fastest-growing sustainable compound earnings growth possible at a significant discount today. Paying two or five or even 10 times today's average market multiple will give you fantastic investment returns *if* you get two, five, or 10 times the earnings growth of the average S&P 500 stock.

In fact, in times of economic expansion, investors should and will pay significant market multiple premiums for rapid and sustainable earnings growth—it's hardwired into our human nature. Let me explain.

HUMAN BEHAVIOR AND PREMIUM MARKET MULTIPLES

There are three rules that control movement of investment capital. All three are closely linked to innate human behavior.

The Obvious-Growth Rule

We know investment capital moves toward the most obvious sustainable growth and away from the least obvious growth. The key word here is "obvious."

But what comprises the most obvious growth sector and the best space? Most aggressive-growth investors with capital to invest seek their answer to obvious growth following this basic line of logic before they invest:

- Where is the fastest, biggest, and most locked-in sustainable growth in the economy today (the largest-magnitude ChangeWaves)?
- Which sectors are the biggest beneficiaries of this huge, predictable, and sustainable growth (the ChangeWave sweet spots)?
- Which companies are best positioned to capture a disproportionate percentage of this locked-in growth? (Emerged and Game-Over Dominator leaders)?

When institutional investors come to what they feel are the most obvious, most predictable, "no-brainer" answers to these questions, they move their capital out of areas that are most predictably at risk of low growth, and move it into the areas of highest or most obvious predictable rates of sustainable growth.

Yes, it is the "obviousness factor," or degree of confidence in future growth predictability, that makes capital move toward or away from a sector or a stock. Once identified, a torrent of money gets aimed at this "strategically advantaged" or positioned space when a majority of aggressive-growth investors come to the same "no-brainer" conclusion. This is what I call a "group blinding flash of the obvious."

The bigger this secular growth opportunity, the larger the amount of cash that will flow toward it. The larger the amount of capital seeking a home within an industry, the higher the market multiples paid for the most strategically advantaged stocks within that sector or space—and the higher they will rise in value.

The 90/10 Disproportionate Reward Rule

To understand why seemingly rational institutional growth investors are fixated on finding and owning the dominant company in what they believe will be huge and rapidly growing markets—and why they will pay astronomical premiums for these stocks once they feel they have found them—remember how you played marbles. In the stock market, as in the marble arena, winner takes all.

Aggressive-growth managers believe in the 90/10 Rule. Ten percent of the companies will get 90% of the market capitalization of the space because, in nine out of 10 cases, the Game-Over Dominator winner *does* take all—all the profits, all the industry valuation, and, eventually, most of the business.

Rajiv Chaudhri, the very successful portfolio manager of the Digital Century Capital hedge fund, explains the groupthink behind this firmly held rule of almost all aggressive-growth investors. And although he primarily invests in information technology companies, the law and perspective he speaks about apply as well in any brain-powered Techonomy industry.

As Chaudhri explains in a May 1999 *Barron's* article: "It is very important to identify the future winners of any potential large market. . . . As markets become larger, the number of really successful companies becomes fewer and fewer, and at the end of the day, there are one or two companies at the most that really dominate and walk away with the bulk of the industries' profits . . . and valuation. We've seen this in micro-processors (Intel). We've seen that in PC operating systems (Microsoft). And in dozens of smaller industries, too."

When investment managers find two or three emerging leaders com-peting within what they consider to be a "soon-to-be-discovered" indus-try, I call this the "Leaders Take Most" play. They buy the emerging dominators with more than 15% market share and let them fight it out.

Once a stock becomes commonly recognized as the No. 1 or No. 2 Emerging Game-Over Dominator in an acknowledged high-secular-growth industry, both stocks will soar until one stock unambiguously dominates the market. In an industry perceived to have years of rapid growth ahead, the winning stock's value is virtually certain to grow to a point where it exceeds those of all the other competitors in the industry combined. For example, in the high-growth storage area networking software space, Veritas and Legato had been vying for dominance. It was a seesaw battle, but in late 1999, Veritas pulled ahead. Shortly afterward, Legato reported very disappointing earnings.

As a result, Legato crumbled in market value and Veritas went on to gain another 100 points. To institutional investors, Veritas is now the odds-on Game-Over Dominator of this 50% to 75%-a-year growth space. As a result of being crowned the Game-Over Dominator, it has a market capitalization value larger than those of all other now-marginal-ized competitors combined.

This behavior is as predictable as the coming of spring and summer. According to Chaudhri, "When the dust settles in any information tech-nology–based industry, there will be one company with 60% to 70% of the market share and the bulk of profits and valuation in that segment. The No. 2 guy will have a 20% share. And the rest? Who cares?"

But why is this winner-takes-all rule so predictable across so many varied industries and decades?

The Human Element Behind the 90/10 Rule

Anything in life that is highly predictable and involves human beings involves innate human nature. Individually, one can achieve changes in personality and behavior. En masse, however, human beings are quite predictable. Evolution is an ongoing, extremely slow process. As a species, we may exhibit greater awareness, increased sensitivity to certain issues, and even flashes of evolving into a more rational and balanced people over centuries and millennia. But in the short term, it's a safe bet that human nature will follow some fairly predictable courses.

Each of us is hardwired to make decisions that we believe will enhance our position, outlook, or longevity. We instinctively seek to make the best of situations in our own self-interest throughout the days, weeks, months, and years, and throughout our careers.

Commerce originated because individuals sought to fulfill human needs. People make choices based on the value propositions that commercial vendors offer. A person's decision to buy from one company versus another and to buy one product or service rather than another boils down to a simple equation:

$$\text{Value} = \frac{\text{Perceived Differentiation from Alternative } \mathbf{x}}{\text{The Emotional Payoff's Relevance to Me}}$$

This equation is a fancy way of saying that every individual is going to judge what is most valuable to him or her based on self-generated criteria. What makes the 90/10 Rule so accurate is that when it comes to just about anything, but especially technology purchasing, most individuals are looking for the same payoff: the lowest-risk solution. In technology, a solution has the lowest risk if it is the most widely used and supported. The lowest-risk solution is not necessarily the best solution technologically—it's the solution that is most ubiquitous. Ubiquity in technology means that the largest technical and operational resources are available to deliver, implement, and support the solution. That's what makes it the lowest risk.

In short, in technology, risk is measured not by risk of technological failure but by risk of operational support and interoperability failure.

This innate search by human beings for the lowest-risk solution, and the inherent logic in technology that the most-used, best-known, most widely supported solution *is* the lowest risk, is what drives the 90/10 Rule to its uniform consistency and accuracy in this and just about every other product or service you can think of.

CASE 1: TALE OF THE TAPE

Betamax and VHS videotape machines were introduced around the same time. From a technical standpoint—as anyone in the television and film industry will attest—Betamax technology is clearly superior. It offers a sharper picture, higher resolution, and a host of other advantages. Yet VHS became the standard.

Why would anyone choose VHS over BETA? Because, among many other reasons, the purveyors of VHS had stronger marketing and stronger distribution, generating more favorable articles in the press, and did a better selling job to national retailers. VHS appeared to be the best-selling format, so it began the self-fulfilling cycle of becoming the video standard. (FYI, it was VHS's early and aggressive move to capture the adult movie industry that put it over the top as the market-share dominator for videotape recording and playback.)

Soon, anyone who wanted to tape the NBA Finals or a favorite movie or create home movies quickly realized that most recorders and camcorders used VHS and most retailers stocked only VHS. What's more, their friends and relatives were using VHS cassettes. It was in an individual's own best interest to purchase VHS cassettes and machines, because it was the lowest-risk solution.

CASE 2: THE DIRTY ON QWERTY

The same phenomenon occurred with keyboards. The QWERTY keyboard is inferior to the Dvorak keyboard. The QWERTY was devised more than 100 years ago to slow down typists. If the QWERTY designer had put the most commonly used letters in the middle of the keyboard, the keys carrying the letters to the paper would jam. With the "a" and the "e" in distant locations and the "n" and the "t" and the "s" away from each other, fingers strike the keys slightly more slowly, thus allowing clunky, manual typewriters to perform adequately.

As technology improved, and later as the entire society adopted PCs, the rationale for QWERTY keyboards disappeared. In the digital age, it flat out makes little sense. Keyboard manufacturers worldwide know this, yet consumers, and institutional and retail buyers, including PC distributors, have stuck with QWERTY keyboards.

Why? They are the keyboards most people learned to type on and so they are the ones they want to buy. QWERTY keyboards became the lowest-risk solution.

INDUSTRY STANDARD

Investment managers understandably gravitate toward companies that have the de facto technology standard in an industry and/or the one-stop, "closed-loop," low-risk-solution provider. In every industry you can name, companies battle to establish the de facto standard. This is also known as the natural monopoly, techopoly, or, in Microsoft's case, your basic monopoly. The winners of these industry standard wars emerge as Game-Over Dominators and their stockholders reap the glory and wealth of the 90/10 Rule.

Cisco, for example, at its peak sold 80% of all telecommunication routers and dominates its niche because it hit a critical mass and became the most predictable solution (a.k.a., the low-risk solution) in its industry. As a game-over dominant standard holder for enterprise routers, Cisco best satisfied the emotional wants and needs of both its customers and its institutional investors.

STOCKS ARE LIKE CORNFLAKES

The 90/10 Disproportionate Reward Rule applies to most nonregional commercial endeavors—not just technology. Why are the most familiar national brands so successful today? First, the human brain can handle only so much stimuli at a time. If I see two boxes of cornflakes on the supermarket shelf and one of them says "Kellogg's," I have a good idea of what I'm going to get for my money. If the other box of cornflakes is the store brand, however nutritious, well-packaged, and competitively priced it is, my inclination is still to buy the brand-name product. While studies show that in many cases store brands exceed the value of brand-name products, they never sell as well.

In a world of rapid change, well-known brands become the touchstone of familiarity, trust, and reliability, justified or not. Well-known brands become the low-risk solution that people, be they investors or consumers, innately seek.

Think of Game-Over Dominators as the leading "brand" for both end-user buyers and stock market investors. Both stock investors and product/service buyers are best-brand buyers, because in the rapidly changing world of technology products and services, the brand you trust as the lowest-risk solution is the brand you buy.

THE POWER OF PREDICTABILITY

Predictability is also a very powerful persuader and brand differentiator, as the following example attests: Say you have children. You move into a new neighborhood, and you are looking for a high school for your freshman son. School A has a track record of graduating 89% of its students to college and 14% to the Ivy League schools. Of course, you promised your dad, on his deathbed, that his grandson would get into an Ivy League school. School B is brand-new, with fabulous facilities and a renowned staff handpicked from the finest schools. It boasts the finest computer system of high school in the country. But it has never graduated anyone to anywhere.

Which do you choose—school A or school B?

At first blush, the fancy new school may be attractive. But I bet if you add the emotional baggage of the promise you made to dear old dad, you'd feel a lot better opting for the school with a proven track record.

The very same emotional issue is faced by aggressive-growth portfolio managers every day. When there are time-tested strategies for picking winning stocks that have proved themselves over and over again, why load up your portfolio with dubious stocks? Who wants all the anxiety, all the uncertainty, when you can go with the predictable formula?

THE SOUND-BITE LOGIC RULE

There is a rule related to the 90/10 Disproportionate Reward Rule. I call it the "sound-bite logic rule," because nobody in the growth money management business has the time or the intellectual bandwidth to consider an investment idea or thesis for more than a couple of minutes.

Now, this might come as a shock to some of you, but most aggressive-growth investment managers have the attention span of the average three-year-old. I have watched this phenomenon for years, and now, after managing millions of dollars myself, I know why this pattern is so prevalent.

With dozens of new stocks coming into a money manager's universe every month, and literally a thousand different variables to juggle every waking moment, the human reaction is to reduce the most current thinking on the great investment puzzles to manageable "story bites."

Because money managers think this way, a company has to reduce the components of its investment ideas to the easiest-to-understand-and-believe story bites.

Since no stock gets going or keeps going without big money behind it, the logic behind any of your ChangeWave stocks has to be easy for the big-money players to come to understand and accept—a no-brainer.

Combine our investment mantra "the right stock in the best space" and the 90/10 Disproportionate Reward Rule. They mean that, when armed with a massive no-brainer secular growth assumption, Wall Street investors will come to the same conclusion you did as to which stocks to buy to pay off their "insight."

PART FOUR

Let's Buy Stocks!

CHAPTER THIRTEEN

Managing Risk: How to Survive and Thrive in the New Age of Volatility

STEP NO. 1: DECIDE YOUR PORTFOLIO ALLOCATION

Before you start buying a lot of ChangeWave stocks, let's first make sure you match your dreams with your stomach.

First, you need to understand that a balanced investment portfolio has stocks, bonds, and funds balanced, as Charles Schwab says, between "core and explore" investments. (That means ranked from lowest-risk to highest-risk money.)

Core ("Safe Money") Conservative-Growth Risk Categories

Bond, mortgage, and income stock investments or funds
Value stocks or funds
Ballast-growth stocks (i.e., growth not tied to expansion of
economy) or funds

Rapid-Growth Stocks ("Explore") Risk Categories

Classic-Growth Industries (20%-plus growth): Game-Over
Dominator space leaders
Aggressive-Growth Industries (40%–50% growth): Emerged space
leaders
Speculative-Growth Industries (75%–100% growth): Emerging
space leaders

In order to live with the up-and-down volatility you get with explore investments, you need to allocate the amount of money *you* feel comfortable with devoting toward these stocks. My rule of thumb is to allocate your investment capital (the money you do not plan on needing for five or more years) between core "safe-money" stocks and rapid-growth "explore" stocks by subtracting your age from 100 and putting that number as a percent into the explore stocks universe. If you are 70, that means 30% in explore stocks and 70% in core "safe-money" stocks.

To decide how much total money you want to devote to rapid-growth explore stock categories, I suggest you take the number of years you are away from retirement and allocate that percentage to the speculative-growth category. Balance the remaining between classic and aggressive growth. Five years to go to retirement means 5%, not 50%, in rapid-growth stocks.

To do this allocation right, you need to categorize your existing investments by this method and then add up how you are allocated now versus how you would like things to be.

Please—before you put a dime into ChangeWave ballast- and/or rapid-growth industries and their leading stocks, perform this simple little self-analysis. It will allow you to sleep much better at night.

STEP NO. 2: UNDERSTAND THAT VOLATILITY IS THE PRICE OF ADMISSION TO RAPID-GROWTH INVESTING

Friends, I'll say it again: Day-to-day stock price volatility is the price of admission to the rapid- or high-growth investment world. If you want the high returns, you are absolutely going to have to accept the concept of wide weekly, monthly, and daily price swings. No volatility, no big 50% to 100% portfolio pops.

So repeat after me. To get high growth, I must learn to:

- Endure the brain damage of higher market volatility by owning ChangeWave stocks I have strong conviction about
- Reduce unnecessary business risk by loading my growth portfolio with the companies in the right sweet-spot space loaded with proprietary intellectual property and the management to dominate explosive, long-term irreversible growth markets
- Reduce unnecessary market risk by balancing my stock portfolio between core and explore stocks according to my "sleep-well-at-night" personal risk tolerance
- Perform my 10-minute economic forecasting strategy every month or so to be on the lookout for radical changes in the economy

How do you know you have matched your dreams to your appetite for risk? The best way I know to judge if you have too much risk in your portfolio for your personal risk profile is the sleep-well-at-night test. If you miss sleep worrying about certain stocks, you have too much money in them.

Simple solution: Wake up and get out of the stocks that made you toss and turn. When you have matched your convictions and your stomach to your portfolio, riding out our modern high-volatility markets is a helluva lot easier.

STEP NO. 3: DECIDE ON YOUR INVESTMENT UNIT

After you decide how much money you want to invest in rapid-growth explore stocks and/or ballast-growth stocks as you head into a slowing economy, you divide that number by the number of stocks you want to own.

If you have $100,000 to dedicate to the explore category of stocks, and you want to own a mixture of 10 classic, aggressive, and speculative explore-rated stocks, your investment unit is $10,000, or 100K/10. If you have $50,000 and you want to own 10 stocks, your investment unit is $5,000. And so on. Knowing your investment unit is important to balancing your money across all risk categories.

Now you're ready to buy stocks.

OK, you're bullish on a ChangeWave and have found the sweet-spot space and leader. Now it's time to buy and sell your stock to profit from your insight.

I fill out a "draft" worksheet detailing my investment thesis for every stock I buy—and I strongly suggest you do, too. Taking a few minutes to write down your reasoning and logic for your investment will pay dividends to you in many ways.

1. It forces you to articulate and think through what you are doing—this point alone could double your investment returns. In just one page, you're boiling down your strategic fundamental assumptions and your business fundamental assumptions and analysis into an investment hypothesis. Many times I find this process alone either (a) keeps me from making a mistake and buying someone else's problem, or (b) enhances my conviction to the point that I buy more shares than I was planning to and add to my profits.

2. The worksheet gives you a record of your thinking to add to your daily "Investing Diary." If you don't keep a daily investing diary,

my strong advice is to start. Keeping a running diary of patterns you observe in your stocks and spaces, as well as chronicling your assumptions and trades, will add 10% to 30% to your profits every year—I promise. Every six months or so, I review every buy and sell ticket I have, and revisit my diary to review my successes and my failures. Most of the ChangeWave Investing process was developed through this post facto diary analysis.

3. Your draft worksheets also serve as a strong dose of courage when the schizophrenic capital markets convulse into a short-term "market meltdown" and your precious company is taking a stomach-lurching beating. I revisit my draft worksheets during every 10%-plus market meltdown. In fact, my advice is to go to your local office supply store and buy a three-ring binder and an A-to-Z index. I simply file my worksheets alphabetically by company name and keep them near my computer for reference and security.

4. Denial is not a river in Egypt—it's you kidding yourself about how great your stock picking is. Your investment worksheets don't lie. They tell the exact story of where your assumptions are right on and where you are missing something. A little self-honesty has made me a much better stock picker.

You can create your own worksheet from the one here, but the easiest way to complete this worksheet is to download the file from Change-Wave.com (it's free).

A WAVERIDER WORKSHEET

The ChangeWave You're Riding. What is it (industrial, corporate, fad) and how far along the S-curve is it?

Killer Value Proposition. What is the new innovative killer value proposition and why is the marketplace purchasing behavior shifting toward it?

The ChangeQuake That Started It. What kind (e.g., regulatory, technological, strategic) of ChangeQuake launched the ChangeWave?

The Sweet-Spot Analysis. Why is this space the sweet spot?

Your Basic Investment Thesis: Why will this ChangeWave space *and* this stock be so much more attractive than the average stock over the next 12 months?

Space Fundamentals

Compound annual growth rate 3–5 years out: _____
Addressed market opportunity 3–5 years out: _____
Avg. gross margin: _____

Company Fundamentals

Forecastable Compound Annual Growth Rate (CAGR). How fast do you expect the company to grow its earnings over the next 3–5 years?

Addressed Market Opportunity. How big will the annual revenue in the company's addressed market be in 3–5 years?

Average Gross Margin. How much does the company make from every sale minus cost of goods sold?

Extra Credit—Discounted Cash Flow Valuation. If you want to get more precise on your valuation estimates, go to www.Datachimp.com and complete their discounted cash flow model. Use consensus earnings projections available from Yahoo.com or Marketguide.com.

CHAPTER FOURTEEN

Buying Stocks Safely and Profitably in Bull, Bear, and Correcting Markets

The original ChangeWave Investing buy-and-sell strategy worked great in bull markets. And since we had not seen a real bear market since 1982, we frankly had very little experience in navigating the treacherous waters.

Boy, are we experienced now. Thankfully our technical analysis–based selling strategy saved us from some of the Techwreck of 2000–2001. But the experience taught us many lessons for the future.

So let's update the basic technical buy/sell/hold tactics we developed and tested over the last 24 months to help you buy and sell your profitable investments *while they are still profitable*. When you add just a few simple technical analysis tools to your ChangeWave fundamental analysis playbook, I guarantee you'll vastly improve your stock-picking results.

In fact, what I've found is that by following two simple but unbreakable technical rules—combined with a pen and ruler for good measure—

investors can avoid almost all the heartache they find when bull markets turn into bear markets.

AT THE RIGHT TIME

We need to expand our ChangeWave mantra a little to make you into a great ChangeWave stock owner. We need to expand our motto "The right stock in the best space wins" to "The right stock in the best space appropriate to the business cycle bought *at the right time* wins."

We've expanded the phrase to include the timing of your stock purchases and sales. Just because a stock meets all your requirements and is a highly rated ChangeWave company does not mean you enjoy monster returns on your investment. The fact of life in the stock market is that *when* you buy and *when* you sell has as much to do with your success as *what* you buy.

Don't worry, this is not going to be complicated. By following two simple rules, which we call the "golden cross" and the "death cross" rules of technical analysis, and combining them with a simple pen-and-ruler technique, you can become a masterful buyer and seller of ChangeWave stocks.

First, another little dab of investment theory.

BULL MARKETS, CORRECTIONS, AND BEAR MARKETS

Most investors consider a "bull market" to have started when one of the key stock market indexes has risen 20% or more off of its most recent low. My definition of a bull market is different. I define a bull and bear market by the actual prevailing evidence of the dominant investor psychology trend: Are investors economic optimists or pessimists?

In declaring a bull or bear market, the only evidence that is meaningful to me is what investors are doing with their money. Are a majority of investors buying and holding stocks, or are they selling stocks? Divining the trend of investor psychology is best measured, I believe, by the simple 50-day and 200-day moving average of the daily closing prices of the two key stock market indexes: the S&P 500 Index of the 500 fastest-growing companies and the Nasdaq Composite Index of Nasdaq-listed stocks.

To me, a bull market means that a majority of investor psychology has shifted to optimism about economic growth for the foreseeable future— that is, the proverbial glass is half full, not half empty. The preliminary technical indication we get that a shift to bull market optimism is coming (in addition to our economic forecast) is when the major stock market indices cross and stay above their 50-day moving average for 20 or more trading days.

In virtually all cases in the last 50 years, a sustainable bull market shift is accurately confirmed when the 50-day Nasdaq Index and S&P 500 Index averages cross their 200-day moving averages in an upward direction. The term I use for the 50-day moving average's upward penetration of the 200-day moving average is "golden cross," which comes from Japanese commodity traders.

Knowing the difference between a bull market and a bear market is very important to aggressive investors in that at least twice a year in bull markets we get 10%-plus downward market price corrections.

Corrections are signs of healthy markets, as I've said. They fix temporary inventory imbalances where short-term traders have more stock than do longer-term investors. Corrections take the short-term froth of the market and serve to return supply/demand imbalances.

In a market correction, the 50-day moving average of the Nasdaq or S&P 500 Index can temporarily move near or below its 200-day price moving average, but it returns back through it within 10 to 20 trading days.

In ChangeWave Investing, we use bull market corrections to add to our favorite stocks or to start new positions in all our categories of rapid-growth explore stocks. Bull market corrections last, on average, 49 days. What makes corrections scary for emerging-industry stocks is that their high valuations get hammered 1.5 to 2.5 times as much as Game-Over Dominator and value stocks. So you need to know the difference between a healthy correction and a move to a much more devastating bear market.

Bear Markets

Every three to four years or so, we have 20%-plus down markets. High-valuation aggressive-growth stock values get hammered up to 50% to 60% or more when bull markets turn to bear markets. In ChangeWave Investing, we use our 10-minute economic forecasting strategy to antici-pate bear markets and to be ready to move our money from rapid-growth stocks to ballast-growth stocks, which suffer much less (and many times appreciate in bear markets).

We now have a simple technical analysis tool that has proven to be deadly accurate in helping you confirm your economic forecast. As long-time ChangeWave investors know, our selling discipline has always used 50-day and 200-day price moving averages as "collars" or levels of sup-port that we look to for selling, holding, and buying individual stocks. But recently I've updated our sell discipline to include the opposite of the golden cross formation, the "death cross," to help confirm that bear mar-kets (and big downward stock moves) are on their way.

When the 50-day moving average for a stock or index moves down-ward through its 200-day and does not return within three to five trading days (10 days for an index like the Nasdaq), we have a bear market for the stock and or the index. It's time to get ready to sell.

We use these moving price averages because they best represent the supply-and-demand behavior of the largest buyers of stocks: institutions. When stocks bounce off of 50-day or 200-day moving price averages, the "bounce" discloses where the "institutional bid" is. This is where the fun-damental analysis portfolio managers like me tell the traders for my funds, "I want to own as much of XYZ stock as we can at this price."

When they don't bounce back, and the 50-day moving average pene-trates the longer-cycle 200-day moving average, in most instances over the last 50 years, the death cross indicates you have serious trouble com-ing—in the market or your individual stock.

The Difference Between Bear Market and Bull Market Corrections

The difference between a bear market and a bull market correction is duration. Bull market corrections average 14% down and last on average 49 days—that is, the number of days between the all-time high and the higher-than-last market bottom low. Bear markets last, on average (in modern times), about five to 13 months and average more than 30% in reductions of index prices.

More broadly, a bear market precedes a peak and downturn in the business cycle—it is a leading indicator that a slowdown-to-recession is ahead. A market correction foresees no such economic calamity.

Corrections are simply what they sound like—temporary digestions of higher stock prices between high- and low-conviction stockholders. In a correction, low-conviction stockholders sell because they think things have gotten as good as they can get. The key part to understand here is that they sell to people who don't buy the sellers' forecast. The new stockholders think better times are ahead for the economy and the company and want to own the stocks they think will best pay off their forecast.

The $4 Trillion Death Cross

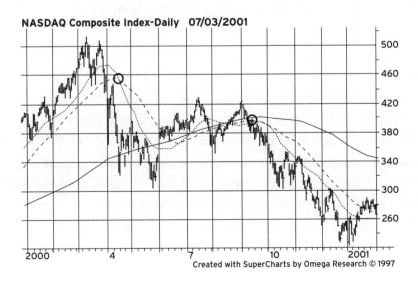

NASDAQ Composite Index-Daily 07/03/2001

Created with SuperCharts by Omega Research © 1997

These new or return high-conviction stockholders absorb the low-conviction stock for sale and eventually correct the market inventory imbalance (i.e., stock for sale vs. bids to buy) that started the downward price correction. In a bull market correction, the market simply consolidates its upward movement and builds a base of high-conviction investors, which will provide the platform for further growth.

Bull markets, as we saw in Chapter 11, are, at their least abstract, a condition where there are more long-term stockholders than shorter-term stock owners. The longer-term stock buyers take stock inventory off the market by holding to their shares. Would-be stockholders who decide which stock to buy on the open market *have* to bid higher for the dwindling supply of stocks—and stock prices continue to trend higher in a positive self-fulfilling cycle.

Bear markets are the exact opposite. Bear markets are a long-term imbalance of too many low-conviction stockholders and not enough high-conviction stockholders. Instead of investors buying on sell-off dips, stockholders continue to *sell* on short-term rallies in a negative self-fulfilling cycle.

USING THE DEATH CROSS AND GOLDEN CROSS TO IMPROVE YOUR BUY/SELL/HOLD PROFITS

Look at the following charts of leading growth stocks. Notice anything in common?

If you did nothing else but buy these stocks after their golden cross formation occurred and sold them after a death cross formation reared its ugly head, I guarantee your investment results in 2000 and 2001 would have been significantly improved. I've gone and back-tested these simple technical formations for 50 years, and they have proven to be the most accurate buy/sell/hold tools I've ever come across.

You should also notice what we call a "mini-cross" pattern on these charts. My back-tested research on tens of thousands of death cross and golden cross formations over 50 years indicates that, in more than 75% of the cases where the 30-day moving average ascends or descends through the 50-day average, the 50-day moving average will go on to cross the 200-day moving average as well.

By adding just these two rules, we improved our buying and selling of ChangeWave stocks by an order of magnitude. I've also added the mini-

$8 Here She Comes!

JDS Uniphase-Daily 07/03/2001

Created with SuperCharts by Omega Research © 1997

"Cisco Will *Never* Drop Below $50"

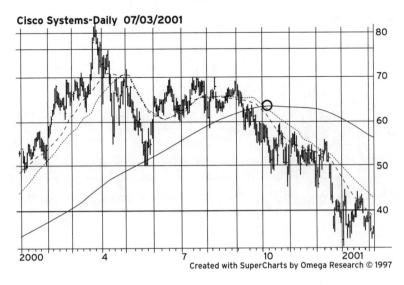

Cisco Systems-Daily 07/03/2001

Created with SuperCharts by Omega Research © 1997

cross strategy to improve our results even more. When we get a mini–death cross on an index or individual stock, I recommend you either close 50% of the position or institute a "good until canceled" sell stop order 3% to 5% under the 50-day moving average to effectively close your position. That

The "Glow" Soon Faded . . .

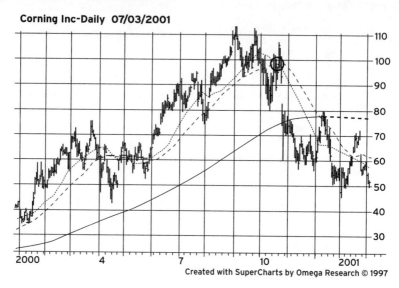

Corning Inc-Daily 07/03/2001

Created with SuperCharts by Omega Research © 1997

Oh Canada!

Nortel-Daily 07/03/2001

Created with SuperCharts by Omega Research © 1997

should be done in advance of the 50-day moving average going on to penetrate the 200-day moving average in a classic death cross formation.

Conversely, when you are in a bull market and the ChangeWave stock you are hunting or already own forms a mini–golden cross, it's time to

Sooner or Later . . .

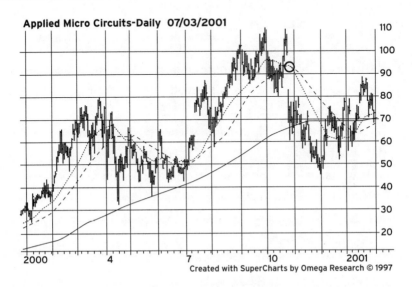

Applied Micro Circuits-Daily 07/03/2001

Created with SuperCharts by Omega Research © 1997

The Death Cross Gets You

Qualcomm Inc-Daily 07/03/2001

Created with SuperCharts by Omega Research © 1997

buy or add to your position in anticipation of a complete golden cross about to happen.

This simple mini-cross technique has added as much as 40% better buy and sell prices in today's volatile markets.

ONE FINAL TECHNICAL CONFIRMATION: THE TREND LINE

Fall a little, rise a lot. Fall a little more, and rise a lot more. Great Change-Wave growth stocks follow this pattern all through their growth period: rise to higher highs, correct or consolidate to higher lows. Using the death cross strategy will help you know when the ride is over and it's time to cash in your profits.

But I always look for confirmation on these death crosses by printing out a weekly chart of the stocks with 30-day, 50-day, and 200-day moving averages and pulling out a pen and ruler. Experienced investors know this as drawing the trend line.

Broken Trend Line Confirms Death Cross

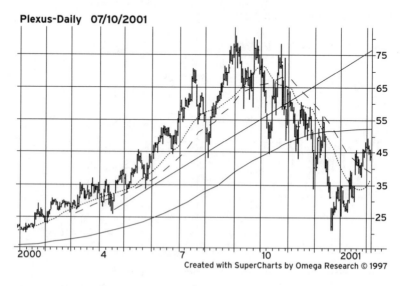

Plexus-Daily 07/10/2001

Created with SuperCharts by Omega Research © 1997

Drawing a trend line is simple:

1. Draw a dot on the three lowest points on your one-year weekly chart.
2. Connect the dots with your ruler and draw a straight line. The dots must cover at least several months.
3. See if the weekly chart of the closing prices has broken the uptrend line.

The idea here is to take a longer cycle than a daily price chart to confirm that a significant change in ownership is taking place with your stock. When you print out the chart, include the weekly trading volume of the stock as well. If the trend line is broken with heavier-than-average volume, this is the final indicator you need to see that the gas is running out of your stock and it is time to take your profits.

Using Trend Lines to Save Your Momo Stock Profits

Let's look at the MicroStrategy chart on page 172. When you have a stock that is skyrocketing up on greater-than-average volume, your stock is in the "Momo zone," as we saw earlier.

The way I make sure I don't leave big profits on the table is to use the stock's trend line to tell me when to sell. When a stock is in the Momo zone, it moves 20% to 40% or higher above its 50-day moving average. This is your first sign. The rule of Momo stocks is this: When it breaks its trend line by closing at a price below your trend line extended past the present day, it is time to sell. If the break comes on larger-than-average volume, sell now.

Trend lines will always help you keep your profits in the Momo zone.

A Meltdown Is Coming

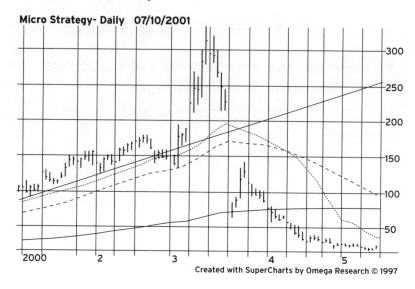

Micro Strategy- Daily 07/10/2001

Created with SuperCharts by Omega Research © 1997

WHY SHOULD YOU WORRY ABOUT THE "TECHNICAL" ASPECT OF AGGRESSIVE-GROWTH INVESTING?

First, great growth stocks move sideways or lower as they move ultimately higher. Without these sideways up-and-down periods of choppiness, called *basing* or *consolidation,* we'd never get rid of the short-term traders and low-conviction stockholders.

Second, successful aggressive-growth investing is a game of owning stocks through higher high prices and higher low prices. The game is won when your stocks move to higher highs than their previous highest price and stop their descents at higher lows. The lower your initial entry price point, the higher your return. Buying low and selling high may sound trite, but it's most definitely the only way you will make money investing in stocks.

All great ChangeWave stocks pause from time to time for profit taking to occur from short-term holders or institutional investors who have to trim their positions to maintain their "investment style" or holding concentration integrity. On any given day, there are a dozen reasons why a big institution has to sell its stock in your favorite ChangeWave company that has nothing to do with the long-term value of the company. Using these simple technical tools helps you to not sweat the day-to-day ups and downs of your stock.

Finally, technical analysis has proved time and time again to help you make more money.

Mark Minervini and his computers at Quantech Research Group have researched the biggest-gaining stocks of the last 50 years (excluding penny stocks under $5), and the results have been validated by the ChangeWave concept since 1995. To wit:

- Virtually all of the biggest-winning stocks started their big moves above their 200-day moving average.
- Ninety-six percent made their move near their 50-day moving average.
- Ninety-six percent of those moves came after a general market correction.
- Virtually all the winners were new companies that had gone public within the last five years and had less than 10 million shares outstanding before their big moves.

SUMMARY

The simple technical tools you have just learned can make a substantial improvement in your profits from stock market investing. Without getting more complicated than a 30-/50-/200-day simple moving-average chart with a trend line drawn with a pen and ruler, I believe you can, more often than not, double or triple your investment returns in the stock market. Not to mention saving yourself the immense and painful heartache of watching a big winning stock give back all your hard-won profits.

None of these rules is foolproof, but my research shows they work far more often than they don't.

Again, if you owned tech stocks with healthy profits in 1999 only to lose those profits (or more) in the bear market of 2000–2001, take a moment to see what using these simple buy-and-sell tools would have meant to your portfolio.

The beauty of being an individual investor is that you can use these tools and act immediately—not like an institutional investor who owns million of shares in the same stock as you. If I get the same signal as you from these tools, it can take me days or even weeks to sell my position out. You can take action in a few seconds.

Get into the habit of printing out your stock charts once a week—it could make (or save) you a fortune.

CHAPTER FIFTEEN

ChangeWave Portfolio Strategies

When you make an aggressive-growth investment, only five things can happen: You can make a large profit, make a small profit, break even, take a small loss, or take a large loss. Only one of these is *not* acceptable.

Our goal in aggressive-growth stock picking in bull markets that accompany economic expansions is to have our winners up eight to 10 times more than our losers. To achieve this goal, we use the discipline of our technical analysis and a few simple portfolio rules to keep the odds of success on our side.

Let's start with some rules for buying rapid-growth stocks in a bull market (or ballast stocks riding against an overall bear market, for that matter):

1. **Buy in a Confirmed Uptrend.** Buy when the market is in an uptrend (as defined by the major market indexes above their

50-day average after the interest rate yield curve has sloped positive) and your stock has at least shown a mini–golden cross.

2. **Buy on a Reversal.** Buy your favorite ChangeWave stocks that have tested but not broken their 50-day moving average or 200-day moving average.

3. **Double Up on the Movers.** Double your position in stocks that have moved 20% higher in three to four weeks or less. According to William O'Neal & Company, publishers of *Investor's Business Daily,* of the 95 top-performing small-cap stocks in 1996–1997 (companies under $5 billion market value), the ones that moved 20% or more in three weeks or less averaged 416% gains over their entire uptrend. Our stock-buying system tries to exploit this pattern by building positions up, and not chasing losing stocks down.

4. **Concentrate Your Picks.** Diversity, or holding 100 stocks in an aggressive-growth portfolio, is the mother of mediocre results. Remember, your goal with your explore portion of your portfolio is to own eight to 10 rapid-growth stocks spread between classic-, aggressive-, and speculative-growth spaces. The reality of investing in a bull market is that only a fraction of the thousands of stocks double or triple in price. In 1999, only 1.4% of the 8,000 stocks that started the year over $12 doubled in value. With your capital spread too thin, you boost the risk of losing out on a huge gain even if you do catch a monster stock. We try to add capital quickly to our winners and get rid of losers or slow performers to concentrate our money in your biggest winners. You are playing the game well when you look at your biggest winners and see that you have the biggest amount of your money in them. You are losing serious money if your biggest-moving stocks have less of your original capital than your less-profitable stocks.

5. **Look for Stocks with Growing Daily Trading Volume.** For a stock to continue moving higher, big mutual funds and hedge funds need to be buying it every day. This requires a great busi-

ness in a great space—our ChangeWave Investing forte. But the way your investment thesis is proved valid is via human behavior—that is, rising volume of shares being traded as our stock trends higher. No higher volume, no sustainably higher prices.

6. **Take Advantage of the Float.** Float is the amount of stock available for purchase. In an emerging growth stock, when lots of investors get excited about the company and there are not many shares available, the limited supply helps drive the price up. Supply and demand works for stocks just as it does for any other service or product.

BUILDING YOUR PORTFOLIO LIKE A BALL CLUB

I like to think of building portfolios as a process similar to building a baseball club. The similarities are pretty striking.

I consider a stock I've bought like a ballplayer I've drafted for my own personal sports team:

* A Minor Leaguer: This is the stock's trial period. If it performs according to my thesis and stays above its mini or complete golden cross line, the position stays and gets more money. If it does not, and drops 8% to 10% from my initial purchase while breaking 30- or 50-day support, the stock is cut from the team. I start an investment in a minor-league stock with a third or half of my desired investment unit amount.

    At the early stages of a new bull market, I prefer to use the ⅓, ⅓, and ⅓ approach to limit my risk by "legging" into a position. I start the investment with ⅓ unit and expect to see a 5% or more pullback from pure volatility. I then add the second ⅓ unit and let the position either move toward profitability (where I add the final leg) or cross and stay three to five days under my technical support line. There I sell it to contain my losses at around 8% to 10%.

In an early- to midstage bull market, I also use a buy-stop order 5% ahead of my initial position to make sure I do not get left behind if the stock catches fire. The buy-stop order, when breached to the upside, coverts to a market order and automatically completes my entire position in a big up move.

Remember, the game here is to have your winners outweigh your losers 10-to-1. This means that for every 10% loss you have a 100% winner. The only way you make this work is to be ruthless about building your initial positions.

- A Major Leaguer: This is a minor-league stock where I have completed my position. Once I have a 10% to 20% profit in the stock, I use a sell-stop order 10% or so under my cost basis to protect myself from unforeseen problems that significantly change the outlook (and value) of the company. This good-until-forbid sell order is my insurance policy against a major loss on an otherwise well-performing stock.

  The stop will not protect you from a severely negative announcement after the close of the trading day. This is a risk you cannot protect yourself from. When one of my major leaguers has moved to a 20%-plus profit, I usually move my sell stop up to my original investment to protect my capital if my cost basis is below the stock's 50- or 200-day moving average. Otherwise I use a "mental stop" and make sure the stock bounces back off any movement below its 50- or 200-day moving average. If the stock swings wildly in one day and I get stopped out (i.e., the stop-sell order price is breached and the broker sells my stock at market) and the problem turns out to be a false alarm, I'll just go back and repurchase the stock. But I have found that this protection strategy has many times saved my butt from investment disaster when one of my companies exposes real problems that radically drop the value of its stock.

- An All-Star: This is a stock that has either made a 20% upward move in three weeks or less since I bought it, or has moved another 20% from its major-league upgrade in less than a three- to four-week period. The idea is to load up on a fast-moving stock before it makes too big a move. There is nothing worse in aggressive-growth investing than to open your portfolio to find your smallest actual investment in a stock that has just made a monster move to the upside. With all-star stocks, I want to double up my investment and overweight the stock vis-à-vis my other portfolio weightings.

Bottom line, the goal of ChangeWave Investing is to put more money into your winners and cut the losers and be done with them. I call this the "Russian Army" approach. In World War II, the supply-constrained Russian generals gave supplies to their armies based on how well they did in battle. If the army won, they would get more supplies. If not, the generals withheld supplies. Now you know why the best Russian armies did so well fighting their way to Berlin!

Ideally, my allocation of cash among my "players"—that is, stocks—is:

- 50% of my money in my all-star WaveRider stocks
- 20% of my money in major-league WaveRider stocks
- 20% of my money in minor-league prospects
- 10% cash

Unless you are comfortable with buying stocks with borrowed money (on margin with a loan from your broker), have a little cash around for a quick-moving opportunity—it has always paid off for me. Sometimes you run out of cash. That's fine.

What this discipline does is force you to make hard decisions on your minor- and major-league stocks. But where do you want most of your original investment capital to be—in a monster stock, up 300%–500%–1,000%, or one stuck at a 60% gain over the same time period?

The key to "drafting" your stocks in a bull market is to get a daily report that shows you:

- A chart of the last 12 months with 30-day, 50-day, and 200-day moving averages overlaid with a trend line you've drawn from the last three low trading points on the price chart
- The average volume of trading over the past 60 days

This data is available at many investment sites, including finance. Yahoo.com, www.BigCharts.com, www.stockmaster.com, and many others.

MORE ON SELLING: MILK THE COWS, SHOOT THE DOGS

Physics teaches us that an object set in motion tends to stay in motion until stopped by an outside force. According to a recent MIT study, high-performing smaller-market-cap stocks (less than $5 billion valuation) over a six-month period tend to continue to outperform the market in the subsequent six to 12 months, while losers continue to lose ground. So we adhere to a strict rule of milking the cash cows—that is, letting the winners ride and quickly pulling the sell trigger on losers at maximum losses of 8% to 10%. Using this discipline adds value to the next rule.

GIVE THE WINNERS ROOM

Studies by stock market academics show that most great growth stocks spend 33% of their time going up or down and 66% going sideways. So we have to give our winners room to win. We do this by watching the 30-, 50-, and 200-day moving averages of our stocks and not reacting to day-to-day swings.

Billionaire tech investor Alberto Vilar once said, "If three of us go to college together and I make As, you make Bs, and the other guy makes Cs, we all pass. Not true in technology investing. Technology stocks get As or they flunk. Now, all I need in a 20-stock portfolio (to seriously outperform the market averages) is three of 20 that are going to become 10-baggers (stocks that have grown to 10 times your original investment). It's weeding out the B students that is the toughest."

Giving room to succeed is especially important if you choose to invest in speculative emerging Techonomy companies. Emerging stocks are much more like venture capital investing than traditional stock market investing because of the valuation paradox we've talked about. Venture capitalists make their big money from only a few of their stocks—but with a few stocks up as much as 20,000% to 40,000% over time, you need only a few.

As I've said several times, the real strategy behind picking monster stocks is to let emerging leader companies grow into Game-Over Dominator stocks—and hang on for the ride. I can't tell you how many times Qualcomm or Dell or Cisco sank to their 200-day moving average but recovered to new highs. The same is true for every monster stock winner I've ever known.

If nothing dramatic has changed in your investment thesis or the company's leadership position in your sweet-spot ChangeWave space, keep your finger away from the mouse. Because the only thing worse than not ever owning a life-altering, monster growth stock is to have owned one and sold it about 10,000% too soon.

COMPANIES LEADING EXPLOSIVE SWEET-SPOT SPACES ARE NEVER CHEAP

Every monster growth stock I have ever owned that was any good never looked cheap and always got ahead of traditional measures of value. Every one. They never were cheap, but when the institutions came to the blinding flash of the obvious I had and "had to own the space and its leaders," the stocks always exploded in value.

Remember that by using the ChangeWave Investing strategies and technical buy/sell/hold protocol, you are doing more strategic thinking and analysis than literally 99% of the rest of Main Street investors—and many of the pros, too.

The ChangeWaves you have chosen to ride, and the sweet-spot space leaders you have "drafted" to profit from your analysis, are certain to be fast movers both up and down in day-to-day prices. But trust your research. The stocks you have selected have a far better chance of going up than do those of other investors who have not done their ChangeWave Investing research.

Based on my six-year 75% annual growth track record, you will win more times than you lose. Your winning stocks will out-earn your losing stocks 7-to-1 on average if you hold your losses to 10% or so per year. This is what I mean by putting the odds in your favor.

BREAKING THE RULES

All selling rules are made to be broken in special situations like these:

1. **Stay through a secondary stock offering.** Give the stock some extra room if the company has sold a secondary or follow-on stock offering. More often than not when a quality company's stock price drops below its 50- or 200-day average when new stock is sold, the stock price recovers when the new inventory is absorbed into the capital markets.

2. **Stay through the acquisitions.** Let the market absorb the news if your company acquires a competitor. Unless the acquisition is completely out of left field or horribly overpriced, the market will absorb it without long-term negative results. In these cases it's just that the market needs a while to become familiar with most acquisitions.

3. **Stay through the lock-up.** In case you own a recent initial public offering (IPO), if your stock goes down, make sure to check if the stock has entered the end of its "lock-up period" (normally six months after the company has gone public). After the lock-up period ends, insider owners are now free to sell their stock. They are no longer "locked up," or not legally able to sell their stock on

the open market. This period normally takes the stock down for a few weeks. But the right stock in the best space usually recovers.

4. **Wait out software companies**. Near the end of the quarter, wait out a dip in a software company's stock until the first few weeks of the new quarter. All software stocks tend to lag at the end of a quarter because their salespeople use the quarter end as a deal closer with their prospects. Predictably, the first month of a new quarter is usually the best for these companies as they start to report their closed deals—and the earnings for completed deals start to hit the books.

For whatever reason, more often than not the right stock in the best space usually bounces off its 50-day or 200-day moving average. Because there are a hundred possible explanations for this phenomenon that defy analysis, I just accept the principle at face value.

Remember, ChangeWave stocks go through consolidation or basing periods more often than they move up or down. As I've said, this is what great aggressive-growth stocks do. They shake out the low-conviction owners and attract higher-conviction owners as evidence of their emerging dominance becomes increasingly acute. You should also count on your stocks taking the scary dives in value during bull markets that come with the normal pattern of roughly every-six-month market meltdowns or 10%-plus market corrections. But eventually, your winner Change-Wave stocks will hit higher new highs and higher new lows.

If you've done your homework, don't get trigger-happy. The day you decide to abandon your discipline and ax your "nonmovers" may be the same day the big news flash hits and your favorite ChangeWave stock makes a 20-point upward upside move.

The only time I sell my major-league stock positions because of slow movement is when I need the cash to double up my position in a new all-star stock that has just taken off. In those circumstances you are being a good portfolio manager. Trading up is concentrating your money in your best-performing stocks. This is how million-dollar portfolios are built.

CHAPTER SIXTEEN

Staying in the Game During Corrections

One of the hardest parts of being an investor in growth stocks is surviving the regular market meltdowns that occur in the technology sector, and the emerging Techonomy industries in particular.

To explain this phenomenon, I turn to the metaphor of a garden. As I dutifully pulled weeds from my beloved flower garden one weekend, I was amazed at how many of the weeds I was removing from my "portfolio" of vincas and pansies did not really look like weeds. A few weeds were even flowering. But we remove weeds to keep our valuable flowers healthy. Regular weeding keeps our really valuable plants healthy, because we know that eventually weeds turn ugly and make our garden less attractive.

The same is true of stocks. Wall Street rightfully establishes a premium valuation on the dominant winners of the long-term-growth industries—the valuable flowers in my analogy. But bull rallies are a lot like a garden on super-high-grade Miracle-Gro. Everything in the rallying sector gets bid up and grows in value—even the weeds. For example, the problem with strong sector rallies like the one we had during the first quarter of 2000 is that every company gets priced as if it were the Game-Over Dominator of its respective market space.

Well, in the stock market as in life, there is only *one* winner in a race. And the network effect of technology in our internetworked world (i.e., the value of a user network goes up exponentially and the number of network participants goes up arithmetically) means that each subcategory of enabling technology eventually does crown one dominant winner.

Game-Over Dominator stocks develop market value in excess of all the remaining wanna-be leaders combined. (The 90/10 Rule shows that the value of the winner's network of users becomes infinitely more valuable than those of its competitors, because it's so much larger than other user networks.)

The painful but necessary process of a violent market correction or meltdown takes down all stocks but ultimately serves to weed out the stocks that are the most overvalued. And which ones are those? The companies that are *not* the dominant players in their industries but are priced as if they are. The overvalued companies are the weeds that look like real flowers but are not.

This weeding-out process is scary to investors but healthy for the bull market. And it should be a lesson to us all about our stock selections. Think of your portfolio as a garden. If you don't weed out your nonleader stocks, they will get weeded out for you in the next regularly scheduled six-month technology weeding-out—a.k.a. a correction.

To be a successful ChangeWave investor you must be able to weather these semiannual market meltdowns. Just as hurricane season comes every year to the U.S.'s Gulf Coast, the high-potential growth stocks that you select will be subject to periodic fluctuations. This clocklike, chilling phenomenon is part of investing.

There will also be times when the entire market takes a downturn. At times, the market is flat out pessimistic for a spell. A company and its stock, however, are two separate things. The growth prospects and potential of a company bear little resemblance to the daily fluctuations of its stock price. The stock market is simply an indicator of people's moods and levels of optimism about the secular growth prospects of the stocks within the market *that day or week.* It is important to understand, however, that the effects of transformational change (ChangeQuakes and the emanating ChangeWaves) don't stop in the face of short-term swings in investor sentiment. Over the longer run, the power of ChangeWaves overwhelms the daily blips of the stock market.

The defining truth about ChangeWave Investing is that ChangeWaves represent fundamental change in how people will behave. With a true killer value proposition born from a genuine ChangeQuake that spawns a powerful ChangeWave, a temporary market meltdown is inconsequential in the long haul.

HOW *NOT* TO FALL PREY TO PANIC

The worst emotional place you can be in as an investor is what I call the Dark Zone. Here you feel actual fear. You panic. You want to sell.

Yesterday, you were a ChangeWave believer. You've done your homework, you've double-checked to see if your technical and economic indicators signal the onset of a genuine bear market—and they don't.

But today, despite all the evidence to the contrary, you believe in getting out of the market as quickly as you can—evidence to the contrary or not. This is the Dark Zone.

If the entire bull market is headed down and pessimism runs amok, it's not out of the ordinary for one or more of your best all-star winning stocks to plummet by half your gains in the stock. Sometimes you'll see this happen over a month or two months in a market correction—sometimes in a few weeks.

Get used to it. Stocks that outperform the market 3-to-1, 5-to-1, or

10-to-1 are the first stocks to get a big haircut when the whole investment world gets nervous and temporarily runs for the exits. In fact, as I mentioned earlier, you should expect the best growth stocks in bull markets to correct 2.5 to 3.5 times the amount of the overall market correction.

If you don't recognize and understand the periodic, but temporary, nature of these market meltdowns, it can suck you into a Dark Zone selling panic that you may regret for years.

Here's a quick way I've found to avoid the panic of the Dark Zone: *Rehearse* the situation before it strikes. What you do is "pre-experience" a situation before it really happens, so that you don't panic in the face of the real thing.

Let's pretend you now own six Emerging Game-Over Dominator stocks and four Game-Over Dominator stocks. Your stocks are up 150% over the previous two years of a nice bull market. Things could hardly be better. Then a market meltdown starts to brew. Market analysts claim there is gross overvaluation in the market. The dollar is getting a little higher. Or there's a hint of inflation.

Suddenly, the news turns bad—a 10%-plus "correction" appears on the horizon. You hear about how the market is heading down. You read that the latest "bubble" is going to burst. When any of these pessimism-inducing events occurs, you must go back to the simple ChangeWave investment thesis you wrote yourself the day you first bought your stocks and read it slowly and carefully. Then go back and reread the Growth Appropriate to the Business Cycle sections of this book and check your economic assumptions and forecast.

Why?

WAVES BEAT STORMS

One night, you find yourself tossing and turning in the midst of a market meltdown. You start thinking to yourself about how you already spent the paper profits you've made on your ChangeWave stocks. You remember the down payment on your condo in Aspen . . . that little Jason will be going to college soon. The next morning you read the paper and come across a pessimistic report on the market, or worse, on the industry and space in which you have invested. Now, instead of the scary words deflecting off you like rain off a raincoat, they begin to sink in. And you succumb. Your fear overcomes your logic. This is when it is absolutely essential that you remember this fundamental point: Genuine ChangeWaves always beat temporary market meltdowns during bull markets.

With your money riding the powerful upward trend of a fast-building ChangeWave, you simply don't need to panic—especially when you've done both your fundamental and economic homework. You have the power of years of research and statistics on your side. In fact, if you hope to achieve the monster gains you are trying to earn, the only thing you must *not* do is panic.

If it helps, when you feel yourself in the panic of the Dark Zone, stop reading the newspaper. Turn off the TV. Stop, temporarily, getting on the Internet and stay away from stock sites. And, sure as heck, don't talk to people who you know will bring you down. Just print out your charts!

Why? Because, paradoxically, the moment that you feel yourself slipping into the Dark Zone is usually the lowest trough of the bull market storm. Not only are you feeling it; everyone else is, too. Remember, human behavior has evolved over thousands of years. En masse, human behavior is both predictable and immutable. When investors slip into the Dark Zone, they panic. And most investors panic at the same things, at the same predictable time. They make irrational decisions. They sell off what would have been perfectly lucrative investments.

THE NO-BRAINER INVESTMENT
STRATEGY AND THE BUSINESS CYCLE

Now that you understand ChangeWave Investing protocol, I'll let you in on a little secret. ChangeWave Investing really just mimics the most pervasive and dominant investment style of our time—what I call "no-brainer" aggressive-growth investing.

We use our concepts of ChangeQuakes, killer value propositions, ChangeWaves, and our investing laws such as the 90/10 Rule of Disproportionate Reward to help us establish what we think Wall Street's most exciting secular growth assumptions are for the real economy of the twenty-first century.

As you know, capital flows toward the most predictable, locked-in places of long-term, rapid growth. That's why growth investing should continue to be the dominant investment strategy of our era. In our increasingly volatile, nonlinear, and rapidly transforming world, human nature drives investors—both professional and amateur—to put their growth money in the surest growth waves they can find.

And in today's world, the surest investment around is stocks, which everyone believes are the primary beneficiaries feeding on the biggest "no-brainer" secular growth stories of our era.

Which enabling infrastructure and understructure industries are the no-brainer winners of the future? The industries with the fastest-growing industrial spaces outgrowing 99% of all other industries in the economy?

This is where the ChangeWave Investing research protocol really shines: helping you identify Wall Street's *next* secular growth assumptions—in other words, the fantastically profitable blinding flashes of the *not-yet-so-obvious.*

Applying our stock-picking protocol simply helps you play the game a few steps ahead of the crowd—and therein lies our advantage.

It's not any more complicated than that.

CONGRATULATIONS!

You've completed the ChangeWave coursework. My hope is that you will have arrived at one of two conclusions. Either (1) the ChangeWave Investing track record is a fluke and not consistently repeatable; or (2)

ChangeWave Investing looks attractive and repeatable—you're ready to get into the aggressive-growth game with some of your investable cash.

I hope you pick 2.

But no matter what your choice, I hope you've come to a few conclusions about what is indisputably new about the world you live in.

CHAPTER SEVENTEEN

The Power of Many, the Focus of One

Indisputably there is an ever-increasing rate of change in our world—which, of course, means an ever-increasing rate of market opportunities. When you stop and ask yourself "How will the world be different by 2005?" the following are virtual certainties:

- The cost/speed of microprocessors will have dropped/improved by at least 1,000%.
- If available bandwidth is tripling every year (Gilder's Law), then we will have 15,000% more telecommunications bandwidth capacity than we do today.
- There will be in excess of one billion users of the Internet.

But those computations recognize only linear improvements from what we know now. If we've learned anything from the Techonomy revolution, it is to expect *nonlinear* change. We're most excited about new discontinuous ChangeQuakes, new resulting killer value propositions, and the resulting highly profitable ChangeWaves we don't yet see but know lie just around the corner.

What's also indisputable about the coming Techonomy is that when we connect the entire world together into one giant knowledge and information database, expecting the unexpected becomes the norm. You should expect nonlinear changes in everything you think is already impossibly fast or impossibly high.

MORE CHANGE

When you free your mind of its linear mentality, the possibilities and potential for the future are startling. What's truly staggering to me is the magnitude of ChangeWave Investment opportunities that lie ahead, if one is to assume that today's frame of reference for change is understated. Today we are extrapolating the future using the reality of today's technology. What if you were to smash that mental prison and imagine the next few years' technology?

University of California Berkeley researchers have a design for a new kind of transistor that is one-twentieth the size of today's smallest transistors—and will lead to chip devices that will store 400 times as much data as today's densest microchips at vastly lower prices.

Molecular-scale electronics is coming—and coming fast. Microelectromechanical systems, or MEMs for short, have the potential to accelerate the power and speed of every part of the information technology "understructure" by *100 orders of magnitude.* Labs today are testing optical switches that would cost 1/1,000 as much as today's highest-speed photonics and are capable of multiplying the speed of the Internet 10,000%. IPv6—the next Internet communication protocol—is on deck. With it you can connect everything to everything. Who knows what killer value propositions this new capability will bring?

The point? Let your mind be free, and watch the change that follows.

YOU DON'T HAVE TO DO THIS ALONE

Charles Schwab and Co. conducted extensive research into the basic style or type of investors. They came up with three major types:

1. **The Self-Directors.** These investors do their own research and analysis, from soup to nuts. Self-Directors are interested in quality research that helps them make up their own minds as to what to buy, sell, and hold. Self-Directors make up about 5% to 8% of the investing public.

2. **The Validators.** These investors have a very good idea about where they want to be investing, and a good idea about the companies that pay off their ideas. But the Validators (for a variety of reasons) are more comfortable getting third-party validation, feedback, and refinement to their ideas before plunking down hard-earned cash. The Validators make up about 30% to 40% of investors.

3. **The Do-It-For-Mes.** These investors do not want to be involved in their investments. They prefer someone else to invest their money so they can do other things. They make up about 30% to 40% of investors.

For those who like the idea of ChangeWave Investing but are true Do-It-For-Me investors, I've established a ChangeWave mutual fund. The Marketocracy ChangeWave Fund invests in the world's most profitable ChangeWaves and sweet-spot space leaders appropriate to the business cycle every day.

But if you are a Self-Director or a Validator, I have great news.

THE CHANGEWAVE ALLIANCE

In this age where traditional "sell-side" stock analysts (those who work for brokerage firms that sell stocks and bonds) are being asked to testify before Congress about the abysmal results from their stock recommendations, their numerous conflicts of interest, and just how they really earn their multimillion-dollar salaries, we have launched a ChangeQuake of our own against the traditional Wall Street "sell-side" analyst world.

The ChangeWave Alliance (CWA) is, in essence, a co-op of credentialed, profiled ChangeWave Investing field experts who spend their everyday professional lives working on the frontlines of Techonomy industries or professions. As in the open-source software world, CWA members, in return for free access to the end-results research of the community, contribute their eyes, ears, and brains to our investment-intelligence-gathering community. CWA members also join one or more space-specific teams we call industrial intelligence panels (IIPs).

Our novel idea is to improve the traditional investment research model by removing the conflicts and roadblocks to gathering and distributing unbiased buy/sell/hold investment advice. In short, we have changed the model of investment research into a team sport.

Our IIPs are organized around many of the emerged and emerging sectors within the Techonomy. The IIP teams are moderated by a ChangeWave.com staff member or IIP volunteer and have one purpose in life: Within their sector, they seek to discover and validate investable opportunities as defined within the ChangeWave Investing research protocol.

What Are the Advantages of the ChangeWave Alliance?

I think the ChangeWave Alliance can significantly improve the odds of your getting rich. Or, if you're already rich, then getting substantially richer. Here's the math behind this bold claim:

More than a decade ago, a brilliant young technologist, Bob Metcalfe, was trying to sell a new networking technology he called Ethernet. He coined the term "Metcalfe's Law" to suggest the unique logic behind the power of a network. As Kevin Kelly describes this math in his seminal work *New Rules for the New Economy*, "Mathematics holds that the sum value of a network increases as a square of the number of members. In other words, as the number of nodes (connections) in a network increases arithmetically, the value of the network increases exponentially."

The Internet itself is perhaps the best example of this "network effect." E-mail wasn't valuable to you until a critical mass of people you communicated with had it. Take the fax. When most people had one, yours became more valuable to you. Now when you buy a fax for $100, you don't just get a piece of equipment. You are buying access to an entire network of 20 million–plus machines. Each additional machine sold increases the value of your machine. In short, in a network, the more plentiful things become, the more valuable they become.

When you add to this calculus the many academic studies that find that the more diverse a group is, the higher the quality of decision making, you start to get the logic behind the power of the ChangeWave Alliance.

In a nutshell, when you apply and are accepted into the ChangeWave Alliance network, the network becomes more valuable to the existing participants. The next invitee who joins makes the network more valuable to you. And so on and so on. Every new member increases the richness and reach of the entire network's intelligence gathering and processing. Each new "node" in the ChangeWave Alliance network raises the odds of the success for all members of the alliance.

Every time we increase the richness and reach of our intelligence, we add another 100 or so investable-intelligence-gathering and -analysis research hours to our system. And every quality research hour we add to the system means we get closer to finding our next ChangeWave sweet spot and, we hope, a few more monster stocks.

But what makes the network work in the context of discovering and communicating "investable" intelligence is its common focus, protocol, language, and peer-review improvement process.

The Power of Many

Whereas other networked investment communities have a group of many but the power of none, we have the power of many and the focus of one. Rather than being the tower of investment babble online or essentially an entertainment media, our ChangeWave Investment Alliance members identify ChangeWaves and help identify Game-Over Dominators and Emerging Game-Over Dominators—to the benefit of everyone in the Alliance.

We restrict the CWA membership to volunteers who are credentialed professionals and subject-matter experts within the Techonomy industries. Laypersons who lack credentialed expertise in the industries we cover simply cannot make the same contributions as those of everyday professionals working in their fields of expertise. Nonmembers, however, can receive our free subscription newsletter (now over 250,000 strong) and receive highlights of the Alliance members' research.

What we're trying to do is create an open-source investing force of the highest level—and the most powerful core DNA, as it were. Limited to qualified members, our investment research improves in the same way that the Linux operating system and Apache software, other open-source systems, have been so successful. Qualified members e-mail in specialized industry information, and as a result the system benefits from a continuous stream of investable intelligence no hired staff of any size could emulate.

The Alliance is more than 2,500 members strong as of this writing. We project the network to grow to 10,000 credentialed members by the end of 2002. Think of the power of 10,000 people—and 100,000 research hours per year—relaying intelligence from hundreds of industries and spaces into one central intelligence-gathering and -analyzing organization!

Ten thousand people who have studied, played with, toyed with, dabbled with, invested in, spoken about, written about, and researched investable opportunities in real-world situations all day long. You can't buy expertise like that. Wall Street can't buy a force like that.

The WaveWatcher Game

We field our industrial intelligence panels to get these best and brightest members all on the same page. Their kick is that their contributions get graded. No kidding. We learned a few of the basics of this concept from the wildly successful open-source portal Slashdot.org, which has turned peer-review critiques into a science. Our underlying rationale is that just because someone has invited you to become an Alliance member (membership is good for one year), it doesn't mean you get to stay in forever. Each member of the Alliance has to earn his or her own keep.

What matters is that all the other members of the ChangeWave investment community are counting on you. We all count on each other. That's why our community is so powerful and unprecedented.

Only those members whose intelligence submissions are graded B or higher by their professional peers at the end of the year are invited to remain in the network. The Alliance does not want the biggest network—we want the smartest.

Why Do So Many Professionals from All Over the World Actively Participate in ChangeWave Investing?

For one thing, you could call it self-interest. The Alliance members know that the more people participate in the network, the greater their chances for catching the next Qualcomm or AOL wave in their portfolio.

There is also the personal recognition factor. Never underestimate the value of braggin' rights among a bunch of Type A people. At the end of each year, we award the "Green Hawaiian Shirt" and significant cash prizes to the WaveWatcher panelists who submit the most profitable ChangeWaves, Aftershocks, or specific company intelligence.

Members also get firsthand intelligence on what's really going on in their industry that are not available anywhere else in their industry. For most members, it's also just fun to be part of a team, of a community wrestling with some of the fundamental questions of the day—what spaces are cooling off, what breakthrough developments are hot. It's fun to reap the rewards—and it's fun to win. And there is an emotional payoff: the feeling you get when you know a space or stock that you helped to identify early on turns into a monster growth stock. Fellow

Alliance members and individual subscribers to Alliance research may be able to send their son or daughter to Harvard because of what your Alliance field report meant to their portfolio. For many, the pride and emotional payoff are just as sweet as opening up your portfolio statement and seeing a new zero added to your balance (OK, almost as sweet.)

Most ChangeWave Alliance members are invited to participate in this open-source investment research virtual community by members who are friends and business associates. You can nominate yourself to be part of the Alliance at www.ChangeWave.com.

So You're Not a Techonomy Professional

For those of you who simply want to get investment advice generated via the ChangeWave Alliance, you can sign up for a subscription to the Alliance. A subscription is available at ChangeWave.com.

THE VISION OF CHANGEWAVE INVESTING

I believe both the future of the single growth fund manager and single investment adviser newsletter editor is limited. The reason? Fundamental technological innovations, or ChangeQuakes, that lead to irreversible ChangeWaves in the economics of capitalism (i.e., the printing press, agriculture, the steam engine, and now global broadband Web connectivity) *always* result in a rapid and dramatic "complexification" of the economy. Always.

To you and me this means we are living through a quantum leap in the number of different economic sectors—as well as the companies within those sectors. The reality of this economic complexification is simple: It is literally impossible for one growth portfolio management team, let alone one single growth portfolio manager or newsletter adviser, to keep up with the magnitude of change and complexity exploding within our real economy.

Until the advent of a single, worldwide real-time communications system this vision was technically unfeasible. But with the advent of Internet-based communication and broadband networking, together with the unilateral investment research language of ChangeWave Investing, it has become technically and practically feasible to launch what we hope becomes a new paradigm for investment research.

CONCLUSION

Whether you are a do-it-yourselfer, a Do-It-For-Me investor, or somewhere in between, no one who chooses to use the ChangeWave Investing system should feel left out of the loop. I firmly believe that should you use the ChangeWave Investing method as outlined in this book you will vastly improve your investment results.

APPENDIX

Advanced Due Diligence

Corporate Wave Rating

If you have significant insight into a specific company, you can use that knowledge for in-depth fundamental research into your favorite WaveRider company.

I use this chart to rate companies in 11 categories. A high score (4 to 5 Waves) in each category is necessary for companies to execute their business model and to plan well enough to become the Game-Over Dominators of their space.

5 Waves = 9 points (excellent; as good as it gets)

4 Waves = 7 points (very good, but not among the best you've ever seen)

3 Waves = 5 points (nothing special; average)

2 Waves = 3 points (lacking; below par)

1 Wave = 1 point (worthless)

1. Intellectual Property (IP) Rating: We give 5 Waves (9 points) to companies with intellectual property that is patented, high-leverage, high-gross-margin, mission-critical, common-thread-enabling information technology. If a company has the intellectual property that has become the de facto industry standard that addresses huge potential markets or has the potential for ubiquity within one or more of the Monster ChangeWaves of the economy, that's sure worth a 9 (think PC operating systems or Qualcomm's CDMA patents).

2. Corporate Carnivore Rating: How big and how innovative is the company's strategy for the future? How willing and able is the company to use merger-and-acquisition to fulfill its vision?

3. CEO Maverick Rating: Revolutions are led by nonlinear revolutionaries, not incremental improvers. How does the CEO rate as a rebel?

4. COO Execution Rating: A great vision without superb execution of the business plan is a tragedy for the company and its investors. How well does the company execute its business model on the field of battle?

5. CFO Earnings and Accounting Management Rating: Wall Street hates surprises. The CFO's job is to manage the company's top and bottom line and Wall Street at the same time. You get a Wave for every two quarters the company has met or beat growth estimates on the top and bottom line. Any accounting shenanigans and the company is immediately off our buy list.

6. Market-Share Position Rating: Number one gets 9 points. Number two gets 7 points. Everyone else gets 1.

7. Corporate Culture Rating: Nothing is more important to executing your business plan in a knowledge-based company than the quality of the corporate atmosphere and the strength of its culture. Great things come from people who want to make a difference and feel like they are allowed to do so. A "Top 100 Places to Work" rating, a below-industry-average turnover rating, or a high score from the ChangeWave Alliance rating gets you 5 Waves. Close to that bar gets you 4 Waves. This is the toughest asset to rate without having direct experience with the company, but it is too important to ignore. Use the CWA rating if there is one.

8. Sales Team/Sales Power Rating: How strong is the sales team? Virtually all Game-Over Dominators have the strongest sales force in their field. Coincidence? I think not.

9. Strategic Alliances/Ecosystem Rating: What connections to Game-Over Dominators in other spaces has the company developed? What is the degree of influence on other companies in the space, and how deep are the relationships they maintain? An investment from a company at the top of the New Economy food chain like Intel, Cisco, or Microsoft is worth 2.5 points.

10. Killer Value Proposition Rating: How far ahead or locked in is the company's value proposition to its customers versus

competitive offerings? This rating must include up to 3 Waves for the uniqueness of the value proposition (i.e., how many others are doing essentially the same thing?) and up to 3 Waves for the degree of gap between competitors (measured in years or patent protection).

11. Wall Street/Media Sponsorship Rating: Who is "pounding the table" on the SuperSpace, and who is pounding the table on the company? Stocks will forever be sold, not bought. The difference today is that stocks are sold by the financial, business, and New Economy media, the company's brand image, and Wall Street "sell-side" analysts. Emerging Game-Over Dominator companies in emerging spaces by definition have little Wall Street coverage but need to have sufficient news flow to feed the adrenaline of short-term investors. Stocks issued by these companies must average at least four significant news releases (contract wins, Alliance wins, design wins, etc.) per month for a 5 Wave rating.

GLOSSARY

Ballast stock: Leaders of industries whose spending growth prospects are not directly affected by economic downturns and are often viewed as "recession proof." A ballast stock lends stability to a portfolio when market conditions are volatile or bearish and are the most appropriate stocks for growth investors in periods of overall economic growth contraction.

Blinding flash of the not-yet-obvious: The moment you discover a powerful ChangeQuake that your research indicates is going to become a highly investable ChangeWave.

Business model:

1. What does a company do?
2. How does a company uniquely do it?
3. In what way (ways) does the company get paid for doing it?
4. How much gross margin does the company earn per average unit sale?

ChangeQuake: A potentially transformational technological, regulatory, economic, or strategic shift or capability within an economy, industry, or individual company. ChangeQuakes are the enabling factor in the formation of a secular wave of new demand/spending or the achievment of new levels of corporate profitability within individual corporations. ChangeQuakes precede the formation of a ChangeWave.

ChangeWave: Shorthand for a rapidly growing, sustainable S-curve or wave of new spending or level of corporate profitability. Metaphorically, a ChangeWave represents the slow-to-fast-to-cresting growth rate and scale of new demand/spending/profitability within an industry or individual company benefiting from a transformation shift (a ChangeQuake) that has occurred within their industry/company.

ChangeWave Alliance: A network of Techonomy industry professionals sponsored by ChangeWave Investment Research, LLC, using the Change-Wave Investing strategy within a broad spectrum of industrial categories, or "spaces." This "distributed-knowledge" community, limited to Techonomy knowledge workers and subject-matter experts, is dedicated to one goal: improved investing results via superior investment intelligence created and delivered every day by ChangeWave Investing systems analysis, logic, and raw intelligence-gathering.

ChangeWave.com: The Web site that supports individual ChangeWave investors and ChangeWave Alliance members.

Dark Zone: The panic attack that investors get during market meltdown periods that drives them to sell their biggest winners to relieve themselves of the "pain" of losing gained profits.

Death cross: A death cross is a trading tool that indicates when a selling trend is under way. This technical indicator is formed when the 50-day moving average of a stock falls below (crosses) the 200-day moving average, indicating that there are currently more people selling than buying the stock than in the past. In ChangeWave Investing, this is a clear sell signal. Fifty- and 200-day death crosses are usually preceded by the 30-day closing price moving average breaking/crossing the 50-day—we call this a "mini–death cross" and use this formation to initiate sell orders.

EBITDA: Earnings before interest, taxes, depreciation, and amortization.

Emerging Game-Over Dominator: The not-yet-dominant leading or coleading market-share company within an industrial space.

Entry point: The price point at which an investor takes an initial position in a stock. Defining an entry point depends on the approach taken when analyzing stock prices—that is, whether an investor is using technical or fundamental analysis. A good entry point for a growth stock is near a bottom of its price range or at a breakout price from a higher high.

FadWaves: A temporary high-growth phenomenon caused by the emergence of a mass-market consumer fad. The killer value proposition behind the FadWave is that it is a new way to be cool (purchase of the product) with an emotional payoff that (for a while) many people can't resist.

Float: The percentage of a company's stocks that is held by the public and not by insiders. A limited supply of stock means more buyers than sellers for recently public Techonomy companies in high-demand, no-brainer spaces. This supply-and-demand imbalance is what rockets these stocks to their first 500% to 1,000% wave of appreciation.

FUD: Fear, uncertainty, and doubt—what most people feel when a new technology or industry threatens their existing world.

Game-Over Dominator: The dominant market-share leader within an emerged market space.

Golden cross: A trading tool that indicates a buying trend is in place. A golden cross occurs when the 50-day moving average of a stock breaks above (crosses) the 200-day moving average. This technical indicator tells you that there are currently more people buying than selling the stock than in the past. In ChangeWave Investing this is a clear buying signal. Fifty- and 200-day golden crosses are usually preceded by the 30-day closing price moving average breaking/crossing the 50-day—we call this a "mini–golden cross" and use this formation to initiate buy orders.

Gross profit margin: The money left after a company pays for the cost of its goods or services sold. We use this screen to eliminate companies that don't have a scalable business. "Scalable" means that the costs to actually produce the service or product should be relatively fixed so that when unit volume hits critical mass, gross profit margins (sales price minus cost of goods sold) stay high or go higher. In ChangeWave Investing, a company with a gross margin less than 50% does not make it onto our team.

Growth Appropriate to the Business Cycle: A capital-preservation strategy within ChangeWave Investing that postulates investing in immature aggressive-growth industries and emerging ChangeWaves is inappropriate during the interest-rate induced contraction phase of the business cycle. Appropriate ChangeWaves for periods of economic contraction come from the ballast-growth industries and ChangeWaves whose spending growth rates are not directly linked to overall economic growth.

Incremental change: Synonymous with linear change—change that improves the status quo. Incremental change or transitions are not investable opportunities.

Industrial intelligence panels (IIPs): Credentialed members of the ChangeWave Alliance empaneled within one or more sector and subsector panels based on their professional expertise, experience, and educational training. The richness and reach of sector and space IIP members are the main intelligence-gathering tools used to collect and review investable intelligence on ChangeQuakes, emerging ChangeWaves, and their sweet-spot primary beneficiary spaces.

Infrastructure: The enabling hardware, software, and services required in the delivery of a technological solution.

Inverted yield curve: When shortest-term interest rates move higher than longest-term interest rates, this indicates the bond market is projecting a downward shift and contraction phase in the business cycle within a 12-month period.

Investment unit: In ChangeWave Investing, investors are urged to divide their investment money ($10,000, $100,000, or whatever the amount may be) into 10 units and then allocate it from there. We encourage people to manage their portfolio risk by allotting money into different sectors. A mature sector has the lowest risk and lowest reward. Immature sectors have the highest risk and highest reward.

Killer value proposition: A new, order-of-magnitude improvement in the status quo, or what is known as the "existing value proposition." Massive shifts in customer demand result when entrepreneurs create and customers adopt new killer value propositions. ChangeQuakes are killer value proposition enablers, the catalyst for irreversible secular shifts or conversions in customer demand and spending.

MarketQuake: Market moving shifts in the bond and/or employment markets. When shortest-term interest rates move higher than longest-term interest rates (a.k.a. an inverted yield curve), this indicates a downward shift and contraction phase in the business cycle (and vice versa). When the economy shifts from creating jobs to losing jobs, this indicates the beginning of a recessionary economic phase where economic growth stalls and turns to economic contraction (and vice versa). We use these two simple indicators to forecast the expansion and contraction phases of the business cycle.

Market meltdown: The clockworklike, once-every-six-months or so sell-off of the technology sector in general. Seasonal money flow and trading patterns make the May-through-October season particularly difficult for high-growth, high-P/E stocks. Once this period has passed, stocks (for a variety of economic and behavioral reasons) blossom.

Market risk: The risk that investors will not be willing to value a stock at current multiples of annualized per-share earnings. Market risk (i.e., P/E multiple expansion or contraction) is a form of investment risk separate from business risk.

Mission-critical common-thread enablers: This less-than-graceful term describes a uniquely and highly profitable type of sweet-spot company that provides a product or service that is:

- Pervasively mission critical throughout many sectors—that is, this company offers a must-have enabling component, application, or service
- Agnostic, taking no sides in the battles for marketplace domination, so they benefit no matter who wins

These companies are the ultimate "bullet sellers"—they make money from virtually everyone.

Momentum zone: When a stock is being violently moved upward by price or earnings momentum investors. Momentum investment strategy artificially makes stocks with positive price or earnings growth momentum move ever higher until the good news stops—then the reverse happens. In ChangeWave Investing, when a stock makes 5%-plus daily moves higher on higher-than-average trading volume, we use trailing stops in order to ensure that our profit is maximized and not lost to the inevitable major price reversal.

Monster ChangeWave: Shorthand for a macroeconomic or economy-wide secular transition. In the U.S. economy we consider a secular macroeconomic transition "monsterish" if its revenue is projected to exceed $1 trillion.

Moore's Law: The thesis, proffered by the cofounder of Intel, Gordon Moore, that the computing power of semiconductor chips would double every 18 months without additional cost. This increasing-return phenomenon is one of the key drivers of high-tech unit growth at lower unit prices.

Moving average: An average closing price for a stock over a fixed time period. The moving average smoothes out day-to-day swings in prices and creates a context in which to judge price trends.

90/10 Disproportionate Reward Rule: In any industry, 90% of the market capitalization of the industry will go to 10% or less of the market participants. This rule validates the premium valuation of dominant leaders of industries that experience high rates of secular growth.

No-brainer: Something that is so blatantly obvious or easy to grasp, virtually everyone gets it.

No-brainer Logic Rule: All things being equal, the simplest to understand secular growth and competitive advantage logic wins the growth stock debate.

Open-source investing: A cooperative network of securities research whereby industry professionals adopt a common investment research logic and analysis protocol. The network shares their collective observations and peer-reviewed investable intelligence. Improvements to the model are incorporated and updated to all participants.

Order of magnitude: A 10-times increase in power, magnitude, or benefit of a product or service.

Price-to-earnings ratio (P/E): Price divided by earnings per share. Literally means the ratio of a company's stock price to its 12-month earnings per share. The standard prism by which stock pickers attempt to value, or "discount," the future earnings of a company. The higher the P/E ratio a company commands, the higher the expectations for future rates of growth.

Pure play: The percentage of a company's revenues within a favored industrial space. Typically more than 50% qualifies, but 75% or more is better.

Secular change: A long-term sustainable or noncyclical transition or trend.

Sell stop: A protective measure that automatically triggers the sale of stock once its price dips below a certain predetermined level. A sell stop is also called a *stop-loss order*. In more detail, a sell-stop limit order means that when a stock falls to the level you have indicated as the point to sell, the stock will be sold at the *exact* price you have specified. (However, remember that a falling stock may not always hit the exact price you have specified. It may jump down and miss your sell-stop level altogether.) On the other hand, a sell-stop market order means that once the stock falls to that price, the stock will sell at whatever the market price of the stock is at the time.

Sweet-spot stocks: The primary economic beneficiary of a demand or spending ChangeWave. Within the value chain of a ChangeWave there is often a company that leads an industry in the supply of an irreplaceable component sold at above-average gross profit margins—this is the sweet-spot "space," and the leading company in that space is the sweet-spot company.

Techonomy: An economy where a 50%-plus majority of its gross domestic product comes from industries primarily addressing the creation, transportation, computing, viewing, or utilization of bits of data instead of physical products. The foundation of this world starts with natural gas being piped into an electric generator that sends power to a data center, plug, or computing device that turns electrons into bits of data. This data is stored, transported on photons, computed, displayed, and added to products and services in the pursuit of commerce, entertainment, and communication. Given the most likely long-term growth rates (averaging 10%-plus a year) of techonomic industries vs. non-techonomic industries (growing about 2%), the U.S. economy will likely become a Techonomy by the end of 2018–2020. This transition represents the third great change in how value and wealth are created within the world's economy and will be the birthplace of most great wealth creation over the next decade.

Trailing sell stop: A trailing sell stop is designed to protect an investor's profits. A standard sell stop is a price below a stock's current price that an investor sets as the sell point for the stock, identifying a bailout point if the price drops too low. However, with a trailing sell stop, the sell-stop price is manually adjusted upward as the stock price increases, guaranteeing that profits will be retained if and when the stock price declines.

Understructure: The raw components used within the enabling hardware, software, and services required in the delivery of a technological solution.

Value chain: An enabling subset of component and services space that enable the delivery of a ChangeWave's end-user solution/service.

Wave Map: A schematic representation of the ChangeWave's value chain identifying the enabling beneficiary sectors of the ChangeWave secular growth assumption.

MORE INFORMATION ON CHANGEWAVE INVESTING

About ChangeWave Investment Research:

ChangeWave Investment Research, LLC, a subsidiary of Phillips International, Inc., is an investment research intelligence network powered by thousands of accredited and organized frontline professionals. In addition to *WaveWire Weekly*, CIR publishes *ChangeWave Investing*, the investment advisory service that helps investors research and discover stocks that profit from radical change, and *ChangeWave ProTrader*, an aggressive trading service that enables investors to manage their money similar to the way professional hedge fund managers do. For more information, or to sign up for the free e-letter *WaveWire Weekly*, go to www.changewave.com.

About the ChangeWave Alliance:

The ChangeWave Alliance is the world's leading Internet-based investable intelligence network. Working together, members of the Alliance discover, analyze, and disseminate advance-notice advice on a wide array of investable growth opportunities. Our goal is simple: Identify the very best companies establishing dominant positions in high-growth areas of the market. The Alliance is composed entirely of credentialed New Economy professionals who spend their everyday lives working on the frontline of transformational change. They are the pros who are relied on to contribute investable intelligence for the benefit of the ChangeWave group. If you feel you are qualified, please visit the site at www.changewave.com/Alliance/intro.html, take a tour of the Alliance, and apply!

BIBLIOGRAPHY

Browning, John, and Spencer Reiss. "Think Locally, Act Globally." *New Economy Watch,* February 2000.

Burnham, Bill. *How to Invest in E-Commerce Stocks.* New York: McGraw-Hill, 1999.

Downes, Larry, and Chunka Mui. *Unleashing the Killer App: Digital Strategies for Market Dominance.* Boston: Harvard Business School Press, 1998.

Drucker, Peter F. *Post-Capitalist Society.* New York: HarperCollins Publishers, 1993.

Du Bois, Peter C. "Chaudhri's Laws—Interview." *Barron's,* May 10, 1999.

Elliott, John. *The Theory of Economic Development,* 4th ed. New Brunswick, CT: Transaction Publishers, 1983.

Evans, Philip, and Thomas S. Wurster. *Blown to Bits: How the New Economics of Information Transforms Strategy.* Boston: Harvard Business School Press, 2000.

Gibson, William. *Neuromancer.* New York: Ace Books, 1994.

Grove, Andrew S. *Only the Paranoid Survive: How to Exploit the Crisis Points That Challenge Every Company.* New York: Doubleday, 1996.

Hamel, Gary, and C.K. Prahalad. *Competing for the Future.* Boston: Harvard Business School Press, 1996.

Hulbert, Mark. "Scary Stuff, Indeed: Halloween as Bellwether." *New York Times,* February 20, 2000.

Hyatt, Joel, Peter Leyden, and Peter Schwartz. *The Long Boom: A Vision for the Coming Age of Prosperity.* Cambridge, MA: Perseus Publishing, 1999.

Johnson, Paul, Tom Kippola, and Geoffrey A. Moore. *The Gorilla Game: An Investor's Guide to Picking Winners in High Technology,* 2nd ed. New York: HarperBusiness, 1998.

Kelly, Kevin. *New Rules for the New Economy: 10 Radical Strategies for a Connected World.* New York: Penguin Group, 1998.

Kelly, Kevin. "Wealth Is Overrated." *Wired,* March 1993.

Laderman, Jeffrey M. "Commentary: We're All Tech Investors Now." *Business Week,* October 25, 1999.

Mandel, Michael. "How Fast Can This Hot Rod Go?" *Business Week,* November 29, 1999.

Mintz, S.L. "The Second Annual Knowledge Capital Scoreboard: A Knowing Glance." *CFO,* February 2000.

Nakamura, Leonard. "Intangibles: What Put the New in the New Economy." *Business Review,* July/August 1999.

O'Neil, William J. *24 Essential Lessons for Investment Success: Learn the Most Important Investment Techniques from the Founder of Investor's Business Daily.* New York: McGraw-Hill, 2000.

Petzinger, Jr., Tom. "The Front Lines." *Wall Street Journal,* January 1, 2000.

Porter, Michael E. *Competitive Strategy: Techniques for Analyzing Industries and Competitors.* New York: Free Press, 1998.

Raymond, Eric S., and Tim O'Reilly. *The Cathedral & the Bazaar.* Sebastopol, CA: O'Reilly & Associates, 1999.

Schumpeter, Joseph A. *The Theory of Economic Development,* 4th ed. New Brunswick, CT: Transaction Publishers, 1996.

Shapiro, Carol, and Hal R. Varian. *Information Rules: A Strategic Guide to the Network Economy.* Boston: Harvard Business School Press, 1999.

Tapscott, Don. *Digital Economy: Promise & Peril in the Age of Networked Intelligence.* New York: McGraw-Hill, 1996.

Thurow, Lester C. *Building Wealth: The New Rules for Individuals, Companies, and Nations in a Knowledge-Based Economy.* New York: HarperCollins Publishers, 1999.

Williams, Roy H. *The Wizard of Ads: Turning Words into Magic and Dreamers into Millionaires.* Austin: Bard Press, 1998.

INDEX

Page numbers of illustrations appear in italics.

C

aggressive investing, 31–32, *32*,
33, 45–46, 90–108, 154, 164
ballast, 45, 92, 94–95, 98, 107,
154, 164
business cycles and, 100–102
capital gains and, 137
case for investing in, 7–16
classic, 98, 154
compound earnings and, 32–33,
46–48
"explore" investing, 33
fluctuations in selling price,
172–73, 187
Growth Appropriate to the
Business Cycle strategy, 90–108
hypergrowth stocks, 49
low-inflation economy and
capital in, 25–26
million-dollar investment
portfolio and, 31–32, *32*
mistakes to avoid, 40–41
monster stocks, 29–30, *30*, 31,
113, 124–26, 141, 181
"no-brainer" aggressive-growth
investing, 189–90
portfolio allocation and, 154–55
price-to-earnings ratio in,
140–42
rapid, 92
returns generated, 31, 33, 38
risk and, 37–41, 97–100, 155
sideways movement of (across
30-, 50-, and 200-day averages),
180–81
speculative emerging, 98, 154
technical analysis, need for,
172–73
time investment in research, 33
strategy for, 46
transformational change and,
48–49

types of investors in aggressive
growth, 126–30
valuations, 130–31, 138–42

H

High-Tech Investing (Murphy), 25
Hypergrowth stocks, 49

I

Inflation, 9
Federal Reserve and, 39, 106
Moore's Law and lowered risk
of, 25
U.S. as highest-profit/lowest-
inflation economy, 23, 36
Information technology
bandwidth and Gilder's Law,
24, 193
corporate capital expenditures
on, 17
cycles in, 96
earnings of employees, 24
growth vs. non-infotech
industries, 18, 19
hurt by Fed's anti-inflation
measures, 26
industries and services set for
growth in the Techonomy, 20–23
microelectromechanical systems
(MEMs), 194
microprocessing, Moore's Law,
23, 193
optical fiber capacity, 24
optical switches, 194
packet switching, 24
patents, U.S. domination of, 24
stock investment, 25–26
U.S. GDP growth, percentage of,
17, 23

Telecom companies, 5, 69–70
Texas Instruments, 83
Tipping points, 53
Trend line, 170–71, *170*
Trends, 62–63

U

Unemployment rate, 107
University of California, Berkeley, 194
University of Michigan Library, Web site for industry newsletters, 80

V

Value investing, 92–93
  ChangeWave Investing as modern form of, 135–37
  Graham-Dodd approach, 137
  intangible asset paradox, 139
  Sanford Bernstein's description of, 136
Venture capitalists, emerging stocks and, 181
Vilar, Alberto, 132–33, 137, 180–81
Volatility, 37–41
  market corrections, 36, 38, 123, 130
  ownership intent and, 123
  rapid-growth ChangeWaves and, 91–92
  understanding and portfolio allocation, 155

W

Warner, H. M., 54
Water management, 30
Watson, Tom, 54
"Wave Wire," 80–81
Wealth-building opportunities
  beginning stages of economic transformations and, 12
  compound growth, 32–33
  doing more with few resources, 13
  future positive for, 11–12
  knowledge and information replaces physical assets, 13–14, 16
  how to get rich off of S-curve transformations, 52–54
  killer value propositions, 73–78, 80
  million-dollar investment portfolio and, 31–32, *32*
  transformational change and, 48–49
  See also ChangeQuakes; ChangeWave investing.
Wealth-creation shift, 12
  industrial revolution, 12, 67
William O'Neal & Company, 176
Williams, Roy H., 74
Wizard of Ads, The (Williams), 74
Worksheet, 157–59

Y

Yield curve, 103–4, *103*
  2001, 104–6

ABOUT THE AUTHOR

Tobin Smith is the founder and CEO of ChangeWave.com, which currently has 250,000 e-mail subscribers, and is vice-president of Phillips International. He is the editor of the newsletter *New Economy* and the managing partner and chief investment officer of ChangeWave Capital Partners, a private hedge fund. A contributing editor at Fox Cable News' *Bulls and Bears* and a regular commentator on CNN and CNBC, he also hosts a weekly chat on AOL and writes for *Smart Business* magazine. He lives in North Bethesda, Maryland.